SHAWN STEIMAN, PH.D.

THE LITTLE
COFFEE
KNOW-IT-ALL

A MISCELLANY FOR
GROWING, ROASTING, AND BREWING,
UNCOMPROMISING AND UNAPOLOGETIC

★ ★ ★

SHAWN STEIMAN, PH.D.

THE LITTLE COFFEE KNOW-IT-ALL

A MISCELLANY FOR GROWING, ROASTING, AND BREWING, UNCOMPROMISING AND UNAPOLOGETIC

QUARRY

Quarto is the authority on a wide range of topics.

Quarto educates, entertains and enriches the lives of our readers—enthusiasts and lovers of hands-on living.

www.QuartoKnows.com

First published in the United States of America in 2015 by Quarry Books, an imprint of Quarto Publishing Group USA Inc. 100 Cummings Center, Suite 406-L, Beverly, Massachusetts 01915-6101
Telephone: (978) 282-9590
Fax: (978) 283-2742
QuartoKnows.com
Visit our blogs at QuartoKnows.com

10 9 8 7 6 5 4 3 2 1

ISBN: 978-1-63159-053-5

Digital edition published in 2015
eISBN: 978-1-62788-322-1

Library of Congress Cataloging-in-Publication Data available

Design: Burge Agency
Illustrations: Laia Albaladejo

Printed in China

THIS BOOK IS DEDICATED TO EVERYONE WHO WANTS TO GROK COFFEE. MAY THE COMMITMENT BE INVIGORATING BUT NOT TOO JITTERY.

INTRODUCTION

PART ONE
THE BEANS

PART TWO
THE ROAST

INTRODUCTION

**THE LITTLE COFFEE
KNOW-IT-ALL**

Why this book?

People are crazy about coffee. They read coffee blogs, trade magazines, and books and attend conferences, trade shows, and coffee schools. They buy all kinds of coffee brewers, grinders, and related paraphernalia. They discuss the nuances of cherry processing, roasting, storage, and brewing at every opportunity. They'll even wait in line for twenty minutes for a $10 cup of coffee! And these are just ordinary people, not coffee professionals!

Coffee has become a worthy hobby and intense passion for all sorts of people. People want to learn as much as they can about coffee and they want answers to all sorts of questions brewing in their heads. What, then, is more appropriate than providing answers to some of those questions in a fun way that doesn't feel too much like a high school classroom? While there are many coffee books available, this one is different. It attempts to look at myriad coffee ideas and explore them using scientific principles, scientifically acquired data, and peer-reviewed publications. Even though the scientific method isn't foolproof and there are other ways of acquiring truth and knowledge, science has generally proven to be a good way of exploring the world.

The scientific method

The scientific method involves learning about a topic, generating a hypothesis, testing the hypothesis, analyzing the results, and drawing a conclusion. This is all done as objectively as possible and according to rules and principles that allow others to scrutinize the process. Science, at its core, is about capturing variation and understanding that variation mathematically. In the natural world, there is variation: Human height varies, leaf weight varies, color varies, sugar levels vary…. By examining many randomly selected individuals in a population, you can get a sense of what the average value for a trait is within that population and how much variation (distance from the average) exists. The more individuals you measure, the better you'll understand that population. As an example, measuring the heights of ten people and averaging them will probably give a poor value for average human height because the variation will be so large. But

measuring the height of 1,000 people will produce much more accurate values of the variation and the average.

Ultimately, scientists ask the question of whether two populations are the same or different. They do this by measuring the average values for a trait in each population and then calculating how much the variation overlaps between the two populations. Depending on how much overlap exists, the populations are considered different (although, different is never absolute; scientists always calculate a probability of making an error). All of this calculating is done using the mathematical field of statistics. Often, scientists create the different populations they are interested in studying. They may add fertilizer to one field but not another or

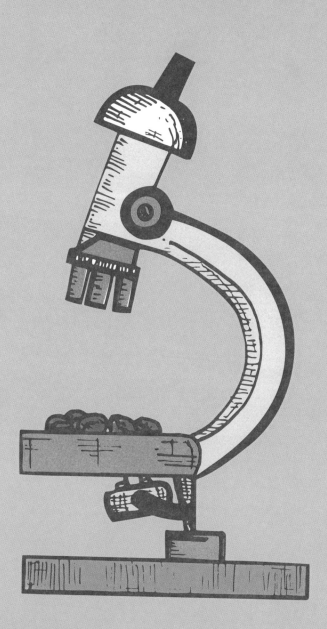

give three groups of dogs different levels of medication. They strive to control all the sources of variation that might influence the populations so that when they finally measure what they're interested in, the difference between the populations is a result of their manipulations, not an event related to something else.

Limitations of science

The scientific method isn't perfect because the world is not simple and scientists aren't perfect. They are human, after all, and prone to all the blessings and curses that entails! There are all kinds of reasons why an experiment may not produce answers that make sense or why one experiment contradicts the results of another experiment. Some experiments, for example, may not be designed and executed well. In other cases, scientists may make mistakes, sources of variation can be difficult to minimize, and some situations are so complex that the experiment may not be able produce unambiguous data. Moreover, complex situations often require the expertise of specialists from different scientific fields or the use of technologies and techniques that aren't yet perfected, none of which may be available to every research team because of resource constraints (time, money, personnel…).

So, science isn't perfect. Still, it has a proven track record (cell phones, vaccines, and space ships are some good examples), and it can help us better understand the world around us. The following pages rely on science, with all its beauty and imperfections. You'll discover that scientists haven't answered all the questions we will be exploring or they haven't answered them very well and, often, we'll have to make some educated guesses to fill in the holes in our knowledge. I'll attempt to be as accurate and transparent as possible, but we may learn something new tomorrow that will make what I've written today invalid. Please, bear with me. After all, I'm just a scientist!

Coffee quality

Coffee quality is discussed and referred to often on these pages. However, because it is a fairly complicated topic, we're not going to spend time discussing what coffee quality means, how we think about quality, or who gets to define what good and bad quality are. Instead, I'm going to proffer a very simple definition that we can use throughout the book.

High quality coffee is coffee that excites coffee geeks. It tends to have acidity and complex flavors that most people don't expect to taste in coffee. Decent quality coffee is coffee that tastes like coffee and not much else. Poor quality coffee has something evidently wrong with it like a moldy or sour flavor.

Disclaimer

All the facts in this book are based on data taken from the scientific literature. In case you want to go to the source yourself, I've included citations that either have the actual data or are review articles that discuss it. I have not included a comprehensive literature review on any topic. Rather, I gathered literature, summarized it for you, and cited some sources that I feel are particularly useful, canonical, or representative. I can't promise I've read everything out there on every topic. In fact, I guarantee it; my command of Spanish and Portuguese and my access to the plethora of literature published in those languages is pretty poor.

There are places and even sections of the book where I take some liberty with statements I make. Every so often, I have to make an educated guess on the science of something for which I couldn't find data.

You'll recognize these instances when you see them, as I use language that suggests doubt or supposition.

Once in awhile, I move into storyteller mode. I tried to make every paragraph relate directly to science and data but it didn't work so well. So, some sections are more background and less science. In addition, some sections are a synthesis of ideas in which I take time to connect the dots, so citing sources for everything wasn't always possible.

Lastly, you'll quickly discover that I've mostly stayed away from the field of medicine. It isn't that there isn't exciting stuff out there about coffee and human health. Rather, it is a topic that is well-covered elsewhere, and I don't want to reinvent the wheel. Also, and perhaps more importantly, I'm not a medical doctor. I'm not very comfortable interpreting data and journal articles, and I would just as soon spare us all the awkwardness of writing about things I know very little about. If you take issue with anything I've written, I welcome you to contact me and engage me in conversation!

PART ONE

THE BEANS

**THE LITTLE COFFEE
KNOW-IT-ALL**

100% ARABICA
★ ★ ★
SO WHAT?

**THE LITTLE COFFEE
KNOW-IT-ALL**

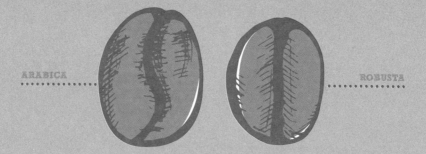

ARABICA • • • • • • • • • • • • • • • •   • • • • • • • • • • • • • • • ROBUSTA

MOST COFFEE SOLD AS SPECIALTY OR GOURMET COFFEE OFTEN IS PROMOTED AS BEING 100% ARABICA. THE IDEA IS THAT THERE IS SOMETHING BETTER (TASTING) ABOUT ARABICA COFFEE THAN OTHER COFFEE. MOST OF THE TIME, THIS IS TRUE!

Arabica refers to a specific species of coffee: *Coffea arabica*. It is celebrated in contrast to its relative, *Coffea canephora*, also known as robusta. These species are the two common commercial species out of the 124 species in the genus *Coffea*. This genus is a member of the Rubiaceae family, which contains the delightfully aromatic gardenia and the unpleasantly aromatic, but purportedly healthy, noni species.

Arabica coffee is the most commonly grown species of coffee around the world. It has always been considered to be the best tasting coffee species. In fact, it is nearly unanimously considered to produce a tastier cup than robusta. So, why would anyone grow robusta, then?

Well, for one thing, there are many positive agronomic traits, and robusta has some that help it grow in different environmental conditions than arabica, in addition to having some very handy disease resistance. Historically, it has been considered easier to grow and more robust (hence, robusta!). Oh, and it has about twice as much caffeine as arabica. So not only does it give your body more bang per cup, but its hardiness can make it cheaper to grow; cheap caffeine is good caffeine.

The differences between robusta and arabica can be a bit surprising once you discover that robusta is not necessarily a cousin of arabica, but possibly a parent! Sometime in the African past, pollen from *C. canephora* or *C. congensis*

The coffee plant is a member of the Rubiaceae family. Quinine, the malaria-fighting drug derived from the bark of the *Cinchona* species, is related.

Kingdom:
Plantae

Subkingdom:
Embrophyta

Order:
Gentianales

Family:
Rubiaceae

Subfamily:
Ixoroideae

Tribe:
Coffeeae DC

Genus:
Coffea

not only landed on the stigma of a *C. eugenioides* flower (the other parent), but helped successfully create a new species which we know and love as *C. arabica* (canephora and congensis are so closely related that we aren't sure which one is the father). Like any child, arabica inherited traits from both parents. Clearly, good taste came from mom's side of the family.

In the United States, most coffee consumed is arabica. However, the lower price of robusta and its bonus caffeine content still make it popular in some market segments where it is blended with arabica. It is a rare event that U.S. roasters use robusta, as it has been demonized as too foul tasting to be considered specialty.

In the past few years, however, some specialty roasters have been exploring the idea that there may be robustas fit for the specialty market, but they must be sought after and discovered. And, farmers need to be encouraged to grow them with the specialty market in mind. The essence of their philosophy is twofold. First, robusta plants have not been treated with the same level of care and attention on the farm and in the mill as arabica has been. Consequently, the unpleasant taste of arabica beans is merely a result of lazy farming and processing, not an inherent genetic roadblock. Second, coffee drinkers have a narrow definition of how coffee should taste and if they expanded their horizons, they will find robustas that are quite interesting and complex. Thus, it is very possible that exceptionally tasting robustas exist, but we have to find them, create them, or accept them as they are. Currently, though, arabica rules the US market and it will be some years before that changes.

WHAT'S SO IMPORTANT
= ABOUT =
HIGH-ALTITUDE COFFEE?

**THE LITTLE COFFEE
KNOW-IT-ALL**

IT IS PRETTY COMMON TO HEAR PEOPLE TALK ABOUT THE IMPORTANCE OF GROWING COFFEE AT HIGH ELEVATIONS. ADVERTISEMENTS FOR MOUNTAIN-GROWN COFFEE DATE BACK MORE THAN FIFTY YEARS, AND COFFEE COMPANIES STILL BRAG ABOUT COFFEES THAT COME FROM HIGH ELEVATIONS. IT MAKES YOU WONDER IF THERE'S SOMETHING MAGICAL ABOUT MOUNTAINSIDES OR BEING FAR AWAY FROM THE SEA.

As it turns out, the scientific data is equivocal on the subject. Some research demonstrates a difference in taste as elevation changes while some does not. Many people in the coffee industry, including this author, have noted that different altitudes produce different cup profiles; coffees grown higher up tend to be more acidy and complex while lower elevations tend to be more intensely coffee flavored. If there really is a difference in elevation, what's going on?

Any athlete will tell you that the air is thinner at higher altitudes. This is because at higher altitudes there's lower air pressure (the weight of all the air that presses down on everything), which means less oxygen is present in any given breath of air since it isn't compressed as much as air at lower altitudes. Plants, however, don't seem to mind this. While nobody has tested the effects of different air pressures on coffee plants, researchers doing space research (astronauts

need to eat, right?) have shown that lettuce leaves changed somewhat when grown in different air pressures. However, none of the research examines the taste. Radishes, on the other hand, barely responded at all to different air pressures (unless the air pressure was very, very low). More interesting, the flavor of radishes and some chemical markers that stand in for flavor didn't change when the radishes were grown in different air pressure conditions. Lettuce (leaves) and radishes (roots) are different types of plant organs than coffee (seeds), so it is hard to draw a strong comparison from these examples. However, considering the nature of the changes in lettuce and the fact that coffee is a seed (organisms tend to be conservative when allowing things to influence their children), it is unlikely that air pressure is influencing the cup quality of coffee.

A change in air pressure is only one of the differences noticed at higher altitudes. The temperature also drops at higher elevations. It has been well documented that temperature affects many aspects of plant growth and

★ ★ ★

"I like coffee because it gives me the illusion that I might be awake."

— LEWIS BLACK —

development across a range of species, including food plants like coffee. As air pressure doesn't seem to be too important in influencing coffee's taste, it is reasonable to assume, then, that the change in temperature at higher elevations is what is influencing our brew.

To support this, we must consider that, across the globe,

temperature is influenced not just by elevation. A major factor is latitude. As the distance from the equator increases, temperatures at a given elevation decrease. So, 2,500 feet (762 m) above sea level in Hawaii is a much cooler climate than 2,500 feet (762 m) above sea level in Colombia. Whereas coffee grown in Hawaii at that elevation can be acidy and complex, it is rarely found to be so in Colombia, even though the elevation is the same. While many factors influence the flavor of a cup of coffee, the temperature at which it grows seems to be one of them. Thus, looking at elevation alone is not very useful, rather, the interaction of altitude and latitude and their influence on temperature is what matters.

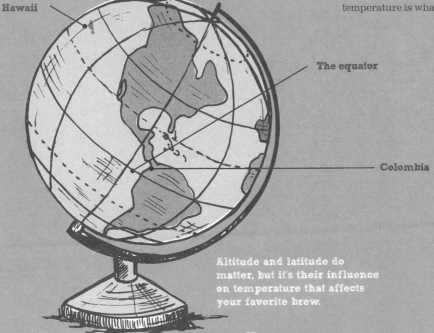

Hawaii

The equator

Colombia

Altitude and latitude do matter, but it's their influence on temperature that affects your favorite brew.

WHAT'S SO SPECIAL
= ABOUT =
SHADE-GROWN COFFEE?

**THE LITTLE COFFEE
KNOW-IT-ALL**

IT SEEMS SILLY TO ASK WHETHER A PLANT NEEDS SUNSCREEN. MOST PLANTS WE ARE FAMILIAR WITH JUST GROW UNDER WHATEVER LEVEL OF SUNLIGHT TO WHICH THEY ARE ADAPTED. IF THE RIGHT CONDITIONS EXIST, THEY'LL GROW. IF THE WRONG CONDITIONS EXIST, THEY WON'T GROW. PRETTY SIMPLE, RIGHT?

Not quite. Humans found coffee growing in the forests of Ethiopia and Sudan. These plants were happy enough with the low light levels of the forest understory. They didn't produce much coffee, but they produced enough that people found it worthwhile to farm the coffee deliberately. For the vast majority of coffee farming history, most coffee was always grown under the shade of trees because farmers struggled to keep plants healthy when they grew them in full sun. With the advent of synthetic fertilizers and then the Green Revolution, farmers discovered they could grow healthy coffee in the full sun. It was easier to grow and the trees produced much more coffee than they did in the shade. How does this work?

Coffee, just like any plant, needs light, just as it needs water, nutrients, and carbon dioxide. Light often serves other purposes in plants in addition to being an ingredient for life. For many plants, light also serves as a signal to the plant. The light quality, quantity, and intensity can all convey information to a plant. This information can lead to a variety of changes in the plant.

Flower production is one factor that seems to be directly affected by light. Coffee plants exposed to lower light levels produce fewer flowers than plants exposed to higher light levels. With more flowers comes more coffee fruit and more coffee seeds. Thus, growing coffee in the shade produces less marketable product than growing the same plant in full sun.

When the plant produces more fruit than it otherwise would because of excess light, it requires more water, nutrients, and carbon dioxide. If nutrients aren't available in sufficient quantities, the whole plant suffers because it can't sustain the nutrient demand of the fruits. Short-term symptoms of nutrient deprivation include chlorotic (yellow) leaves followed by premature fruit ripening, then leaf and fruit drop. When this happens, not only is the current harvest affected, but the next harvest is as well. The only way to recover is to stump or heavily prune the trees and forego any harvest the following year.

So, in the shade of trees, coffee produces a small amount of fruit that can be sustained by the available nutrients. The only way to successfully grow coffee in full sun is to supplement the soil with sufficient nutrients (more water is needed, too, but the increase is smaller). When synthetic fertilizers became available, farmers realized they could grow coffee healthily, easily, and profitably in full sun. While full-sun coffee can also be grown successfully in an organic coffee production system, it is difficult and expensive. Thus, most farmers who grow organically have shade trees to help mitigate the plant's nutrient needs.

In summary, full sun coffee produces more coffee than shade coffee but it requires more inputs to make it successful. Actually, it isn't that simplistic! Having or not having shade trees completely changes the agricultural and biological system of a coffee farm in all kinds of ways. Shade trees interact with the soil by adding nutrients via the decomposition

Shade trees completely change the biological makeup of a coffee farm in all kinds of ways.

of leaf litter, holding it in place (thereby preventing erosion), producing root exudates, and possibly bringing water from deeper regions to higher regions via hydraulic lift. Farms with a larger diversity of shade tree species tend to harbor a great deal of biodiversity, from ants to birds, whereas full sun farms tend to have relatively little biodiversity. Shaded systems encourage some pests

and diseases while suppressing others. Also, shaded systems tend to have fewer weeds (since weeds tend to be sun-loving). Finally, shade trees can provide additional resources to farmers, like firewood or food.

There is also the question of whether shade (or light) has an influence on the flavor of the coffee. There is a romantic notion that because shaded coffee ripens slower and it can be part of a harmonious, complex, biodiverse system that it will taste better than coffee grown in full sun. The available data is noisy, meaning, some research shows a bit of a difference in taste while other research shows no difference in taste. Thus, one can interpret the data both ways. Taken all together, this scientist (who has done research on this very topic), concludes that the amount of light in which a coffee grows has no influence on its taste.

So, does coffee need sunscreen in the form of big trees? No, it can do just fine without it, so long as the farmer is able to supply it with the resources it needs. There are, however, many reasons why a farmer might choose to cultivate their coffee under shade trees. Optimizing potential yield, though, is not one of them.

COFFEE IS
★ ★ ★
THE SEED OF A FRUIT?

THE LITTLE COFFEE KNOW-IT-ALL

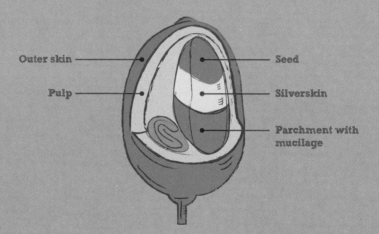

Outer skin ——————— Seed

Pulp ——————— Silverskin

Parchment with
mucilage

THE FUNNY THING ABOUT SUPERMARKETS IS THAT EVEN THOUGH THEY MAKE OUR FOOD VERY ACCESSIBLE AND MORE AFFORDABLE, THEY ALSO TEND TO OBVIATE OUR NEED TO KNOW ANYTHING ABOUT WHERE OUR FOOD COMES FROM AND HOW IT IS PRODUCED. CONSEQUENTLY, MOST PEOPLE PROBABLY HAVE MINIMAL KNOWLEDGE OF PLANTS, PLANT PARTS, AND HOW THOSE PARTS PRODUCE SOMETHING WE CAN EAT. WHEN IT COMES TO COFFEE, IT IS EVEN LESS LIKELY WE'D KNOW ABOUT ITS ORIGINS, ESPECIALLY SINCE MOST OF US DON'T LIVE IN THE TROPICAL LOCATIONS IN WHICH COFFEE IS PRODUCED.

The coffee that we drink is made from a seed found inside a fruit that grows on a shrub (or tree, if you let it grow big enough). The fruit, botanically a drupe, is often red when ripe (some varieties ripen to yellow, orange, or pink). Coffee fruits are often called cherries because they are approximately the size and color of fresh cherries (*Prunus avium* and *P. cerasus*). In between the seed and the outer skin are four other layers: the silverskin, parchment, mucilage, and pulp. All these layers have corresponding scientific terms that allow botanists to compare the seeds and fruits of different species to each other. In botanical lingo, the parts of a coffee fruit are called the embryo (this is what actually becomes the plant; the first leaves to emerge are called cotyledons); endosperm (the major part of the seed that acts as an energy and nutrient source for the embryo once the seed germinates); integument (the silverskin, which is a very thin layer covering the seed); endocarp (the parchment, which is the innermost layer of the fruit); mesocarp (the mucilage and pulp/flesh—this is typically the edible part of most fruits); and epicarp (the outer skin).

Since coffee has a mesocarp, it seems fair to wonder whether or not it can be eaten. Yes, it can! If this is the case, why don't we ever see the fruit in the market place? The answer is that the fruit just isn't all that tasty.

Coffee fruits are not very tender and thus require a good deal of chewing to break them down. They are a bit bitter and a little astringent, though less so than an unripe banana. They are sweet, particularly the mucilage, but not sweet enough that you'd want to eat them over an apple (though if you remove the fruit and just suck on the mucilage, which adheres to the parchment, the sugar intensity is quite high and pleasant). While there's even a little bit of

★ ★ ★

"I have measured out my life with coffee spoons."

— T. S. ELIOT —

caffeine in the fruit (0.36 to 1.3 percent of the fruit weight), it isn't enough to be convincing. The unremarkable taste isn't unreasonable, really, as humans have spent time selecting for good tasting coffee seeds, not good tasting coffee fruit.

This isn't to say people haven't tried many ways to make use of the fruit. I've heard lots of stories of kitchen experiments: coffee fruit wine, beer, pie, smoothies… Yet, nobody has seemed to have found anything that is worth producing on a commercial scale. Researchers have even looked into using the fruit as cattle feed, but that didn't take, either.

Up until recently, the only thing the coffee fruit is regularly used for is as an herbal tea. In fact, historians believe the fruit was consumed as a beverage before the seed was. When the fruit is dried, it can be rehydrated with hot water to produce a mild-tasting, fruity beverage. Currently in the United States, it can be found at various specialty coffee

roasters, sold under the fancier name of *cascara*, a Spanish word meaning "shell" or "husk." Some retailers blend it with other herbs to increase the taste complexity of the final beverage.

In the past decade, the coffee fruit has come to be seen and used as a nutraceutical. The fruit is high in anti-oxidants and companies have begun extracting these compounds for use in a myriad of medicinal products. Coffee fruit extracts have appeared in beverages, pills, and skin creams.

If we consider other foods we eat, it really isn't a surprise that the coffee fruit doesn't have much gustatory value. There are very few examples of foods where we eat both the flesh of the fruit and the seed. Why should this one be any different?

IS ONE ROUND PEABERRY
= BETTER =
THAN
TWO FLAT-FACED BEANS?

THE LITTLE COFFEE
KNOW-IT-ALL

BEAUTY IS IN THE EYE OF THE BEHOLDER. AT LEAST, THAT'S HOW THE SAYING GOES. WHEN IT COMES TO PEABERRIES, THOUGH, IT JUST MIGHT BE TRUE. THE TRUTH IS, WE DON'T REALLY KNOW.

Inside the coffee fruit, two seeds typically develop. As the seeds enlarge and mature, they push against each other. The result of this pushing is the flat face of a coffee seed. On every coffee tree, a percentage of the cherries contain only a single seed. With no opposing seed in the cherry, the lone seed has no flat face. Rather, it is entirely round, almost pealike. This seed is called a peaberry. The percentage of peaberries on a given tree varies, but most of the time it is 4 to 8 percent. There have been several reports, however, of trees that produce percentages from 30 to 35 percent.

Why peaberries occur is not known, though many scientists over the years have speculated on a variety of possibilities. These include genetic factors, plant age, climatic conditions, poor pollination, and nutritional deficiencies. Scant research exists that examines any of these potential influences. Ultimately, some kind of malfunction occurs at the cellular level, which prevents the growth of the seed. The malfunction could occur prior to fertilization. For example, the pollen tube—an organ that grows from a pollen grain after it has landed on a stigma and whose purpose is to deliver its gamete to the receiving gamete in the flower's ovule—might be disrupted, preventing it from delivering its package.

Another possibility is that the gamete reaches its destination, but either the female egg or the ovule itself are inviable, preventing fertilization. Alternatively, fertilization may occur without incident, but the zygote or ovule aborts, leaving an empty chamber behind.

What has become clear is that there is a strong genetic component to peaberries. Offspring can produce different percentages of peaberries than their parents. Irradiating seeds with neutrons or X-rays, then letting them grow into plants, increases the percentage of peaberries. Even manually cross-pollinating flowers decreases the occurrence of peaberries.

Peaberries have captured the imagination of coffee drinkers who seem quite happy to pay a premium for them and roasters are just as happy to supply them. This suggests that there is something different or special about the physiology, biochemistry, or taste of peaberries. Unfortunately, there isn't much research on the subject. Peaberries germinate just as often as their flat-faced brethren. There are studies that show some biochemical differences in the seeds when they are unroasted, but those differences largely disappear after roasting. As for taste, no research, complete with statistical analysis, could be found comparing flat-faced seeds to corresponding peaberries. In the literature where their taste is discussed, peaberries are considered to taste the same or inferior to flat-faced seeds, though the research was just anecdotal.

An important consideration with peaberries and taste is how they respond to roasting. A round, somewhat uniform shape will interact with heat differently than an asymmetric shape. If the heat transfer during roasting is different between the two shapes, resulting in different roast profiles, then a taste difference could arise. If this is the case, then the taste difference is an artifact of roasting, not the internal characteristics of the seed. I hypothesize, then, that the taste difference would be fairly small and nothing of the scale usually touted by retailer or consumers.

With the potential of no important difference, do peaberries warrant their higher price? As peaberries do only occur in low percentages, they are rare; typical supply-demand curves would suggest a higher price. In addition, while farmers have no control over their occurrence, their maximum potential yield is never reached. Each percentage increase of peaberries results in a 0.5 percent decrease in potential yield. This is just a numerical difference. Peaberries tend to be smaller and weigh less than most flat-faced seeds, making the yield, as measured by weight, even lower! Thus, farmers have a sense of being penalized by nature and are keen to make up for the economic loss. Finally, at mills where the peaberries are removed manually, there is an added cost of labor for that effort. Although, large mills with lots of equipment typically have machines that sort coffee by size, separating out the peaberries, and these mills incur no additional cost or effort.

Ultimately, it doesn't matter if there is a statistically significant difference in the biochemistry or taste of peaberries or whether they cost more to produce. If consumers continue to pay a premium for them and believe them to be better, then they are better, at least in the mind of the buyer.

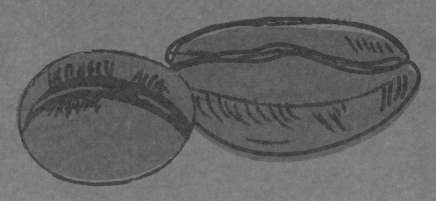

WHY DOES MY ROASTER TALK ABOUT CHERRY PROCESSING?

★ ★ ★

THE LITTLE COFFEE
KNOW-IT-ALL

AS THE COFFEE SEED IS THE PART OF THE COFFEE CHERRY THAT INTERESTS US THE MOST, WE HAVE TO EXTRACT IT FROM THE FRUIT AND GET IT TO A POINT WHERE IT CAN BE ROASTED. ESSENTIALLY, ALL THE LAYERS MUST BE REMOVED AND THE SEED NEEDS TO BE DRIED DOWN FROM ITS APPROXIMATE 50 PERCENT MOISTURE CONTENT TO 9 TO 12 PERCENT MOISTURE CONTENT. WE CAN THEN DISCARD (OR FIND A USE FOR) THE FLESH AND OTHER UNWANTED LAYERS. THUS, CHERRY PROCESSING IS A CRUCIAL STEP IN GETTING COFFEE INTO A MUG. WITHOUT IT, THE COFFEE WILL NEVER BE READY FOR INTERNATIONAL COMMERCE.

Exactly how that happens is less important than doing it well. The pulp and mucilage are high in water and sugar content—two attractive resources to microorganisms whose overabundant presence during drying is suspected of negatively impacting the cup quality of the coffee. Minimizing or eliminating their growth is a key aspect of cherry processing. Ultimately, individual farmers decide how to process the cherries depending on the available resources, cost of processing, the climate at the time of processing, the potential of a price premium, and/or the desired taste outcome.

There are three common methods of cherry processing: natural, pulped natural, and washed. There are variations on these but to go into them all is overwhelming. We'll stick to these three.

In the natural process, also known as the full natural or the dry process, the entire fruit remains intact while the seeds are dried. The seeds are not removed until every layer, including the seeds, has been dried. On farms where coffee is harvested mechanically, many cherries are already dry when the coffee is harvested. These cherries, sometimes called raisins, can be separated and sold as natural coffee.

The pulped natural process is one step removed from the natural process. The cherries are pulped (the skin and fleshy pulp removed) and the seeds, still covered by the parchment and mucilage, are dried. This process sometimes goes by alternate names, but "honey" is the most common.

The washed process (a.k.a. the wet process) removes not

Did you know?

On average, about 100 gallons (378.5 L) of water are required to produce 20 grams (0.7 oz) of roasted coffee, enough to brew about one 11-ounce (325 ml) cup of coffee.

only the skin and pulp but also the mucilage before drying down the coffee. There are several ways of doing this. Traditionally, the mucilage is removed by fermentation, either by covering the coffee with water until the mucilage is degraded or simply leaving the coffee to sit and ferment without water (known as dry fermentation). The term "fermentation" is used because microorganisms, naturally occurring on the coffee or in the environment, consume the mucilage and degrade it via metabolic fermentation processes, though microbial enzymes also play a role. When the mucilage is completely degraded and removed, we deem the fermentation process complete. The fermentation

process takes as few as six hours and as many as forty-eight to complete, though typically it lasts twelve to thirty hours. The time required depends on the volume of coffee, ambient air temperature, and temperature of the water (if present) used for soaking.

An alternative method uses a demucilager/demuculator to mechanically remove the mucilage just after pulping, eliminating the need for any kind of fermentation before drying. A demucilager forces the coffee into a small space, causing the seeds to rub and push against each other and the sides of the container. The pressure liquefies the mucilage, allowing it to be washed away in a few minutes by the small amount of water added to the

★ ★ ★
*"Coffee is a
language
in itself."*

— JACKIE CHAN —

process. Since water is used to rinse the coffee seeds upon completion, we call these coffees "washed coffees." Whether a washed coffee is fermented or demucilaged, the cup quality tends to be similar.

It is well accepted by both the coffee industry and scientists that processing affects the cup profile. A generality on perfectly pampered and accomplished processing on farms where hand-harvest methods are used is that going from washed to pulped naturals to full naturals creates an increasing intensity of sweetness, fruitiness (ferment to some), acidity, and body. Some people suggest that the coffees become increasingly complex through this progression.

On farms where coffee is mechanically harvested, the results of perfect dry processing on cup quality aren't as predictable. Natural processed coffees from these farms can be more acidy and fruity than washed coffees, or they can be earthy and/or spicy.

A big question that is largely unanswered is, how does cherry processing affect coffee quality? What is happening, biochemically, to create such organoleptically noticeable changes in the same batch of seeds? Many people in the coffee industry proffer that the sugars and "fruitness" of the mucilage and pulp diffuse into the seed. Unfortunately, this hypothesis lacks any scientific data to support or refute it.

There is not much data to address what is going on with flavor as a result of processing. Moreover, there is as yet no data linking specific coffee chemistry (green or roasted) to organoleptic quality. So, even when changes in coffee bean chemistry are demonstrated, there is no evidence to support that those differences are causing the tastes we experience.

The same coffee processed by different methods will present different amounts of a variety of cellular molecules, dependent upon the processing method. Also, differences in coffee bean metabolism have conclusively been shown between washed and full natural coffees. It is not unreasonable to hypothesize that pulped naturals might fall somewhere in the middle of these differences.

Two metabolic responses have been demonstrated. One is that the seed begins its germination sequence almost immediately after being picked. If the presence of germination-specific molecules (isocitrate lyase and β-tubulin) is measured in coffee shortly after picking and daily until the seeds reach 12 percent moisture, differences are seen between seeds that are fermented and seeds that are naturally processed. In washed coffees, the amount of these molecules peaks a couple of days after harvesting and drop significantly in about a week, whereas in natural coffees, the quantity of those molecules peak a week after harvesting and slowly decline for another week or so. Two factors explain

There are three common methods of cherry processing: natural, pulped natural, and washed. Notably, there is little data addressing how processing affects flavor.

these patterns. The first is that coffee pulp has inhibitors that slow down the germination process. Second, washed coffees dry quickly and, consequently, quickly reach a state of cellular quiescence. Full naturals, with greater mass and higher water content, require more time to dry down to that quiescent state.

The second response is related to water stress. Natural processed coffees accumulate a much larger amount of γ-aminobutyric acid (GABA), a molecule known to occur in water-stressed plant cells. As explained earlier, this disparity exists because the natural processed coffees remain metabolically active for a longer time than the washed coffees.

These responses indicate a significant amount of metabolic activity that is captured by just a few molecules, and the actual changes within the seeds go much farther than just these molecules. It is reasonable to hypothesize that the differences in flavor from different cherry processes stem from these metabolic processes. Yet, until more research is done, we can only hypothesize as to whether the flavor comes from seed metabolism, a migration of compounds into the seed from the mucilage and fruit, or both.

CAN YOU TELL ME THE
FLAVOR PROFILE OF
★ THE COFFEE FROM ★
LOCATION X?

THE LITTLE COFFEE
KNOW-IT-ALL

THIS IS A QUESTION THAT EVERYONE ASKS AT SOME POINT. THE WINE INDUSTRY, THE GRANDDADDY OF ALL SPECIALTY FOOD INDUSTRIES, HAS SPENT ITS LIFETIME BUILDING ON THE IDEA THAT WHERE A WINE IS GROWN, REGIONALLY, IS NECESSARILY RELATED TO ITS FINAL TASTE. THE TERM USED TO DESCRIBE THIS IS *TERROIR*. IT IS A FRENCH WORD MEANING "LAND" BUT ALSO "THIS SPECIFIC LAND" OR "LOCAL". IN AN AGRICULTURAL CONTEXT, IT REFERS TO EVERYTHING THAT PLAYS A ROLE IN THE PRODUCTION OF A CROP—INCLUDING SOIL, CLIMATE, AND TOPOGRAPHY. THE IDEA IS THAT THE GESTALT OF A PLACE IMPRINTS A PRODUCT AND THAT THE PRODUCT, NO MATTER WHERE ELSE IT IS PRODUCED, WILL NEVER TASTE QUITE THE SAME ANYWHERE ELSE; THIS IMPRINT SUPERCEDES THE EFFORTS OF ANY INDIVIDUAL FARMER. THE COFFEE INDUSTRY (AND TEA INDUSTRY AND CHOCOLATE INDUSTRY) TOUTS THE SAME THING: PLACE IS IMPORTANT. IS IT?

To answer this, it helps to first understand all the different things that can influence the taste of a coffee on the farm. Well, coffee is a bit unusual in that some relevant post-harvest events occur that deserve to be considered. So, let's consider all the events leading up to the point where coffee can be roasted, as this is where it is a stable, tradable product.

As has been discussed elsewhere, within the English language, peer-reviewed scientific literature, the following things have been proven to influence the taste of coffee: genetic make-up, elevation (with some equivocation), pests/diseases, cherry processing, drying,

sorting, and storage. Notice the things we haven't researched/can't research, don't seem to play a role, or don't have enough information to draw a conclusion on their effect: light levels, health of the tree (having sufficient nutrients and water), soil type, source of fertilizer, exposure to agrochemicals, plant age, and harvesting (though nobody believes this isn't acutely important). A cynical way to summarize our knowledge at this point is that we don't really know how to produce a good cup of coffee, rather, we just know how to avoid screwing it up.

It certainly seems to be the case that where and how a coffee is grown influences its taste. Thus, there is a terroir for an individual farm. Is there a terroir to an entire growing region, though?

There are seven categories of things that influence a coffee's taste, each having multiple variations, some of which might interact with each

Did you know?

Coffee drinking has no effect on the risk of prostate, stomach, ovarian, and pancreatic cancers. It seems to reduce the risk of liver, kidney, endometrial, head and neck, breast, and colorectal cancers, but it may increase the risk of bladder cancer.

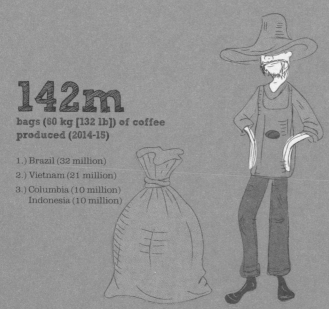

142m

bags (60 kg [132 lb]) of coffee
produced (2014-15)

1.) Brazil (32 million)
2.) Vietnam (21 million)
3.) Columbia (10 million)
   Indonesia (10 million)

26m

coffee farmers

87

countries

Source: Internal Coffee
Organization

> **— Did you know? —**
> There are many ways to go from the fresh coffee seed
> on the tree to a dried, green coffee bean. Each of them will
> influence the quality of the coffee.

other, and nevermind the other items we're agnostic about but might need to be moved up in importance. That's quite a few potential influences. For the idea of terroir to hold true, then all these things must interact in such a way as they can never be duplicated anywhere in the world. Currently, at least eighty-seven countries produce coffee to some extent (not all of them are commercial producers) and most of them have multiple regions growing coffee. Let's say ten regions per country for the sake of our discussion. The International Coffee Organization estimates there are some 26 million farmers in the coffee business, which, even if that were broken into six-member families, would leave 4.3 million coffee farms on the planet. With eighty-seven countries, each with ten regions, distributed amongst 4.3 million farms, the number of farms per region is 5,977. Using these values and assuming every farmer within a region is doing the exact same things to their farms, for terroir to be true, there would have to be 5,977 unique coffee flavor profiles on the planet that are recognized by tasters.

That's a pretty large number. While it is possible to generate that many combinations of flavors based on the seven known factors mentioned above, it seems unlikely that there is that much nuance in the world of coffee. Even more difficult to believe is that all the farmers in a single region—even a single mountainside—are farming in the exact method.

This last idea seems the most relevant to me in this discussion. If all these factors can influence a cup of coffee and each farmer has the freedom to farm and process their coffee as they choose, it is very likely that the coffee from individual farms in a region are going to vary from each other. If this is true, how true can terroir be?

I submit that regional terroir for coffee is an artifact of logistics and we are quickly leaving it behind. The artifact is that for most of coffee producing history, all the coffees from various farms within a region, sometimes even a country, were blended together. This blending occurred post-harvest at the wet mill or at the dry mill. When so many individual farms' coffees are homogenized like this, the taste of the end product will be some kind of average that accounts for all

the coffees that went into it. Then, those coffees were stored and shipped together (not always so well), giving them time to change and equilibrate even more because of the time it took to get them to roasters elsewhere. Terroir, then, was an artificially created phenomenon that arouse out of the logistics of coffee processing, storage, and shipping, not out of the inherent magic of the climate, topography, and farming.

This might just be a semantic argument because it is perfectly reasonable to let logistics be represented in the taste of a place. Yes, at one point, coffees from a country or region in a country probably had consistent flavor profiles and in places that still operate in such a way, these profiles, likely still exist. However, the past few decades have seen diversification in the coffee industry which suggests coffee terroir is no longer true.

One of the hallmarks of the specialty coffee industry is the celebration of individual coffee farms. Coffees of a particular

variety, from a particular farm, that used a particular processing method can be easily found at specialty coffee roasters. These coffees are celebrations of diversity within a particular place. Roasters are seeking and finding coffees that they want to be different from the region's norm. If these special coffees can be found, how can there be an overarching influence of place on the cup profile?

The reality is that two farmers, separated by just a fence, can produce very different coffees. If this is the case, which one represents the terroir of the region? If there are hundreds and thousands of farmers in a region, all able to do their own thing, then who gets the honor of having their coffee be the poster child for the region? As more and more farmers are able to keep their coffees apart from farmers in their region and strive to produce a rare coffee, the potential of terroir being true falls dramatically.

WHY DOES A COFFEE PLANT PRODUCE CAFFEINE?

★ ★ ★

SO MANY OF US LOVE COFFEE BECAUSE OF WHAT CAFFEINE DOES FOR US. WITHOUT THE CAFFEINE, HUMANITY MAY NEVER HAVE CONTINUED CONSUMING COFFEE AFTER THE FIRST INITIAL TRIES. (WHAT REASON WOULD WE HAVE HAD FOR STUMBLING ON THE IMPORTANCE OF PROCESSING, DRYING, ROASTING, AND BREWING?) BUT, WHAT DOES CAFFEINE DO FOR THE COFFEE PLANT? AFTER ALL, IT DOESN'T MANUFACTURE THE STUFF FOR US AND IT REQUIRES ENERGY (AN IMPORTANT COMMODITY FOR ANY LIVING ORGANISM) TO PRODUCE IT.

Discovered in 1819, by German chemist Ferdinand Runge, the caffeine found in the coffee plant plays a useful role, just not a critical one.

Caffeine is considered a secondary metabolite. As opposed to primary metabolites, secondary metabolites are not essential for plant growth and development. Rather, they play some useful role, just not a critical one. Caffeine is found in all parts of coffee, from the roots to the seeds and even in the xylem, the upward-elevator organ in plants. A number of hypotheses have been posited for what caffeine can do for the coffee plant. It could be an allelopathic agent, an anti-herbivory agent, a form of nitrogen storage, and/or a pollinator stimulant.

Allelopathy is plant chemical warfare against other plants. Some plants produce chemicals that can harm or kill seeds or plants, typically of other species. These compounds, spread by the decomposition of leaf litter or exudation by roots and seeds, influence the population dynamics of plants within a community; not all allelochemicals kill all plants. Many researchers have demonstrated that caffeine is toxic to a number of different plants. However, nobody has demonstrated caffeine's efficacy in a natural setting. Thus, just because it can kill some other species, there is no guarantee that it would kill competitor plants in the forests of Ethiopia (where it evolved).

Caffeine is incredibly toxic to some insects and fungi (humans, too, in a high enough concentration). So, it often argued that it is a defense mechanism from critters. This hypothesis is supported by the fact that caffeine is produced in young, developing organs that are more susceptible to insect attack. This is a logical hypothesis but it is incredibly difficult to prove. To prove it inconclusively would require two nearly identical coffee plants, with the only difference being that one produces caffeine while the other one does not. Unfortunately, we are technologically incapable of producing these conditions, so the experiment will have to wait awhile. If caffeine did evolve to protect against insects, it was probably targeted against specific African insects. If it had been successful in defending against them, then they are probably so inconsequential as pests that they haven't ever caught the attention of researchers.

Since caffeine has been found moving up through a plant and it contains four nitrogen atoms, it is thought that it may simply be a way to store nitrogen until needed for a specific purpose. What little research has been done on this hasn't successfully demonstrated this function.

Lastly, caffeine may be an incentivizing treat for pollinators, particularly honeybees. Research has shown that honeybees' long-term memory is improved after having caffeine. Presumably, this would help the bees remember the flower they were enjoying and be more likely to return to it in the future, thus helping the plants to cross-pollinate. While this is promising research, it has yet to be tested outside the laboratory. In addition, it wouldn't explain why caffeine is synthesized in all the organs in the plant.

We will probably never know why coffee first developed caffeine. If we're lucky, we'll find out why it has continued to do so. Of course, from the coffee's perspective, caffeine production has been a huge success. After all, because of that molecule, the human species has spread the seeds of the plant to nearly every place on the planet in which they could thrive!

COFFEE
= CAN =
RUST?

THE LITTLE COFFEE
KNOW-IT-ALL

WHEN THINGS RUST, IT IS ALWAYS METAL THINGS—IRON, ACTUALLY. PLANTS CAN'T RUST AND COFFEE IS NO DIFFERENT. COFFEE LEAVES, HOWEVER, CAN TURN RUST COLORED AND WHEN THAT HAPPENS, IT'S NOT A GOOD SIGN. WHEN COFFEE RUSTS, IT IS BECAUSE A FUNGUS, *HEMILEIA VASTATRIX*, HAS ATTACKED IT AND THE FUNGUS IS SPORULATING, OR PRODUCING SPORES THAT WILL MOVE TO OTHER LEAVES AND INFECT THEM.

There are many diseases that infect coffee, but none are as prevalent and difficult to control as this one. (Coffee Berry Disease is pretty horrible, but it is still contained to the African continent.) Almost every coffee producing region in the world has Coffee Leaf Rust (*roya*, in Spanish), and they all struggle with controlling it. The rust attacks the leaves and turns off any activity in a leaf where it touches. Very light infections simply reduce the photosynthetic ability of a leaf. As infections become more intense, leaves die. If many leaves on a plant are heavily infected, then the plant can lose all its leaves and any fruit that is maturing since there are no leaves to sustain the fruit. The fungus doesn't actively attack the coffee we drink, it just prevents us from ever having coffee to drink.

There are some fungicides that can be used to combat the fungus. However, they are expensive and have to be applied multiple times throughout the season. For small farmers (which make up the vast majority of coffee farmers worldwide), the cost alone can be prohibitive. For farmers with larger tracts of land, the cost is not inconsequential. Moreover, many farms are planted on steep, mountain slopes that are difficult to walk on. Imagine the difficulty of walking on a steep slope and spraying a pesticide at the same time!

With fungicides being a poor option, the best solution is to plant varieties that are (at least somewhat) resistant to the fungus. Unfortunately, there are no pure arabica lines that are resistant. In the 1930s, by a highly unlikely fluke of nature, a natural cross between *C. arabica* and *C. canephora* occurred, producing the offspring known as the Timor hybrid. This plant, having genetic lineage of both species, was resistant to the rust. Once it was discovered, it became the center of several breeding programs around the world. While the disease resistance was a nice inheritance from its canephora parent, it also inherited some of the undesired taste attributes. So, the breeding programs tried not only to improve its agronomic traits but its quality traits, as well. Over the years, other hybrids were discovered or made.

These hybrids were, over many generations, bred with pure arabica lines to further improve their taste. Now the world is populated with many of these breeding program offspring.

The taste of these offspring has never managed to equal that of a pure arabica line, no matter how many backcrosses have occurred. Still, these offspring are rightly called arabica varieties because so much of their genetic material comes from the arabica species. Currently, there are some recent releases that show a great deal of promise in offering rust resistance and desirable quality.

Unfortunately, as with any disease, resistance is not a cure. The fungus is constantly mutating and adapting. Many strains now exist that can attack not only some of the hybrids but pure *C. canephora* lines, as well. So long as coffee is a crop, we will be in constant flux with this and other diseases. It isn't particularly fun or joyful, but it is the way of life.

It was a hybrid featuring the genetic lineage from both Arabica and Robusta plants that became the savior for breeding more rust-resistant coffee plants.

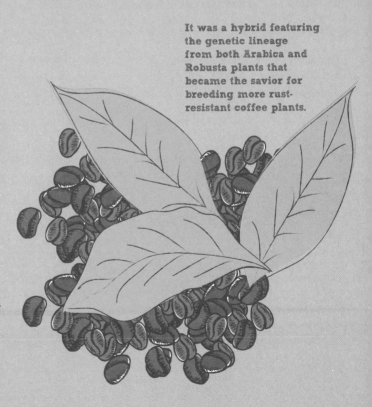

HOW DO I REALLY KNOW
★ ★ THAT'S ★ ★
KONA COFFEE?

THE LITTLE COFFEE
KNOW-IT-ALL

THERE ARE TIMES IN LIFE WHEN YOU WANT CONFIRMATION THAT THE CONTENTS OF A PACKAGE REALLY MATCHES WHAT IS ADVERTISED ON THE OUTSIDE OF THE PACKAGE. IS THE OLIVE OIL REALLY FROM ITALY? IS THE SPARKLING WINE REALLY FROM CHAMPAGNE? IS IT TRULY MANUKA HONEY? THE REASON WE WANT TO KNOW THESE THINGS IS BECAUSE THESE PRODUCTS ARE ALMOST ALWAYS MORE EXPENSIVE THAN THEIR ALTERNATIVES.

Thus, if we're going to pay more for them, we want to be sure we're getting exactly what we pay for (the issue of whether they taste as good as they're supposed to is a topic for another section). How do we prove the product is what it claims to be? Is the coffee really from Kona, Hawaii?

In a perfect world, rare, special, or expensive coffees would taste so different that we'd be able to verify their origins upon tasting them. But, being able to taste with that level of precision is difficult and it requires extensive knowledge of coffees from all over the world. Moreover, every coffee

grown within a particular place must have a shared and globally unique taste. Well, these prerequisites are never all met simultaneously, so, using taste to confirm the origin of a coffee will never work.

Alternatively, a government can establish rules and laws for packaging and labeling and expect its citizens to follow them. Most governments do this and they do their best to enforce them with the limited resources available to them. However, there are always clever miscreants, and a government's power doesn't exist past its borders.

What is needed is an

objective, product-based method for determining where a coffee was grown. All one has to do is discover the right chemical or combination of chemicals that will fingerprint a growing location. If every fingerprint is unique, then one just has to analyze any sample, match it to a fingerprint, and voilà!

Sounds easy, right? The actual lab work is usually fairly easy but discovering a fingerprint is incredibly tricky. Many scientists, including this author, have worked on this problem. Nobody has figured it out yet. There are two big hurdles to this problem. One is settling on the right fingerprint and the other is being able to properly analyze the data to ensure everything works correctly.

Scientists have tried all kinds of different analytical techniques and markers to build the fingerprint: near-infrared spectroscopy (NIRS), fourier transform infrared spectroscopy (FTIR), high performance liquid chromatography (HPLC), solid phase microextraction—gas chromatography—time of flight mass spectrometry (SPME-GC-TOF-MS), brewed coffee volatiles, stable isotopes, elemental content, molecular compounds, and who knows what else! The aim has been to find a very quick, cheap, reliable method that can detect the right markers.

Most of these methods and chemical markers suit this purpose well and much of the data is very promising. The data is promising because many of these methods allow the detection of many signals or markers rather than a small handful. They can be 2,000 reflectances of light at different wavelengths, hundreds of volatile compounds, or dozens of molecules. The more markers one has to create a fingerprint, the more likely that fingerprint will be unique. Moreover, the current state of computer power and statistical software packages allows for adequate analysis of all the data, so building a fingerprint and testing its efficacy is relatively simple.

So, where's the problem? The problem is twofold. One, there are never enough samples in a dataset to build a truly robust fingerprint. Two, any given bean is, well, complicated!

Large datasets are

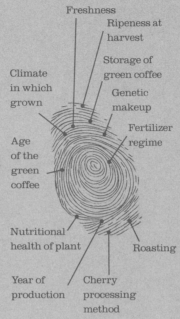

Freshness
Ripeness at harvest
Storage of green coffee
Climate in which grown
Genetic makeup
Fertilizer regime
Age of the green coffee
Nutritional health of plant
Roasting
Year of production
Cherry processing method

important for statistical power and simply being able to paint the right picture. The statistical analysis used in origin discrimination work requires many samples for the analysis to work well. Many studies do the analysis with too few samples and the numbers crunch well, too well, really. The end result is too perfect because so many markers are being used to describe a small set of samples. The data is overfit. Painting the right picture is just as important. If you want to be able to tell a Hawaiian coffee from a Costa Rican coffee from a Rwandan coffee, you need many samples from each location to capture the variation from that

location. Now, with eighty-plus countries in the world growing coffee and each country having many individual regions, acquiring enough samples to paint the big picture is daunting.

As for coffee being complicated, there are just so many things that influence coffee's chemical composition. These include, but are not limited to, year of production, the genetic makeup, the climate in which it grew, the nutritional health of the plant, the fertilizer regime, ripeness at harvest, cherry processing method, storage of green coffee, age of the green coffee, roasting, blending, and freshness. In order for a geographic fingerprint to work, it must be able to account for all these compositional influences every year across many locations!

I believe we have the knowledge and capability to build a geographic indicator system. It may never be perfect but it probably could be effective a very high percentage of the time. All we need are time, manpower, and adequate resources.

In the meantime, how do we know where the coffee in our cups is actually from? Trust. Trust in all the people whose hands touched that coffee and belief that they acted with integrity.

THAT COFFEE WAS
= EATEN =
BY AN ANIMAL?

**THE LITTLE COFFEE
KNOW-IT-ALL**

AS THE STORY GOES, WHEN THE DUTCH FIRST BROUGHT COFFEE TO INDONESIA FOR COMMERCIAL PRODUCTION, THEY FORBADE THE LOCALS FROM DRINKING THE COFFEE THEY WERE GROWING. THE LOCALS DISCOVERED THAT A LOCAL ASIAN PALM CIVET (*PARADOXURUS HERMAPHRODITUS*) ATE THE CHERRIES BUT DIDN'T DIGEST THE SEED. IN FACT, THE SEED PASSED THROUGH THE DIGESTIVE TRACT AND OUT THE OTHER END. THE SEEDS COULD THEN BE WASHED, THE PARCHMENT REMOVED, ROASTED, AND PREPARED LIKE ANY OTHER COFFEE.

Independent of the accuracy of this story, this coffee, known as Kopi Luwak (kopi = coffee, luwak = the civet), has become a coffee phenomenon. Its rarity and consequently exorbitant price has made it a product often talked about and sold in high-end markets. Though, due to its price, few people have probably tried it.

Reactions to the idea of Kopi Luwak are wide ranging, as you might imagine. Few people are keen on the idea of consuming anything that successfully passed through an animal. Yet, others think the quality is significantly different and the social cache, certainly, can't be disregarded. Most members of the specialty coffee community are vehemently against the coffee for its idea and its taste. As one notable industry expert once said, "Kopi Luwak is coffee from assholes for assholes."

Independent of public opinion, there's more reason to ponder the source of the beans. While the initial offerings of the coffee certainly came from the droppings of wild animals, the dollar signs and popularity led more than a few proprietors to start keeping civets in cages and feeding them almost exclusively coffee cherries. While this isn't very different from the way some chickens and cows are raised in the United States, it struck a chord with consumers and became a lively news story for several weeks. Perhaps the idea of an expensive luxury item coming from caged animals was simply too unsavory.

The real question is whether Kopi Luwak is actually different than coffee processed in a more traditional manner. Does the trip through the gastrointestinal track actually modify the seeds in a noticeable way, whether chemically or organoleptically? Fortunately, several researchers have addressed this question and all have come to the same conclusion. Yes.

All the reports I read demonstrated that Kopi Luwak coffee is chemically different than normal coffee. Most of the time, this was demonstrated by measuring the composition of the volatile compounds of roasted coffee, though some research looked at a variety of other physical and chemical markers instead. In addition, two studies concluded that the taste of the Kopi Luwak was different than normal coffee.

While this all sounds very exciting, the researchers,

unfortunately, were faced with some challenges that I'm not sure they were aware of and their data, though interesting, may not be as conclusive as anyone would like. A critical step in doing any experiment is to hold all variables constant except the one in which you are interested. In not a single study was this done. None of them were able to take the coffee from a single tree—even a single farm—and ensure it was processed normally and via civet. Instead, they acquired commercially available samples or samples from within a region. As we learned in the

previous section, just about any history or process can influence the chemical composition of coffees, especially the volatiles. We have no way of knowing whether the differences they found were from the actual processing or from any number of things such as genetic make-up, fertilizing regime, storage conditions, or age.

The challenge of acquiring perfect samples is immense, for certain. Without using a caged civet, it would be impossible to get proper samples. Their efforts should be commended, but the data should be taken with a healthy dose of wariness. Nonetheless, there are some aspects of the data that push me to think there is an actual chemical difference between Kopi Luwak and normally processed coffees.

This applies, too, to the quality assessment of the coffees. Actually, those results are even more difficult to accept as the quality of the sensory analysis leaves quite a lot to be desired.

Independent of whether the coffee is truly different, there is plenty of room for consideration of the animal welfare issues and whether or not any coffee is worth such a high price tag. Like all things coffee, though, it is up to the consumer to decide and nobody else!

Civets are small, nocturnal mammals native to tropical Asia and Africa. They are not true cats, but the civet family is related to the cat family.

PART TWO
THE ROAST

THE LITTLE COFFEE
KNOW-IT-ALL

WHY IS A COFFEE BEAN
= JUST A =
TINY TEST TUBE?

GREEN (UNROASTED) COFFEE IS NOTHING YOU'D EVER WANT TO CONSUME. IT IS HARD ENOUGH TO BREAK A TOOTH, AND ITS TASTE LEAVES AN AWFUL LOT TO BE DESIRED. IN ORDER FOR IT TO BECOME SOMETHING WE CAN GRIND AND BREW, FIRST IT MUST BE ROASTED. ROASTING COFFEE, AS IT TURNS OUT, INVOLVES SOME PRETTY COMPLICATED CHEMISTRY.

When we visualize chemistry, it is quite common to picture a laboratory with test tubes and various pieces of equipment. Mix the contents of two test tubes together and bam! Something new is created! Rule number one about chemistry: if chemicals aren't in the same space physically, then they can't react with each other. Rule number two: sometimes, chemical reactions need a little help getting going and being sustained. This help can come from external energy (heat, typically) or an enzyme (a molecule that facilitates chemical reactions without being used up in the reaction and without requiring much, if any, energy to push the reaction forward).

Roasting coffee satisfies both those rules. The bean itself is the laboratory and the cells that make up the bean are the test tubes. The cell walls and the material within the cells comprise the raw ingredients of all the chemical reactions that take place during roasting. Roasting provides the energy source that begins and sustains the chemical reactions. While there are enzymes of all sorts in the cells, their role in the creation of what we know of as coffee is poorly understood. Most likely, enzymatic reactions don't play a significant role in producing the coffee we know and love.

Actually, a coffee cell is more than just a test tube—it is also a pressure cooker. Plant cell walls are thick and durable. Thus, when the contents strive to get out, they cannot do so easily.

Weight Loss

Volume

Very Light

First Crack (395–405°F [202–207°C])
More acidity, lower body, more complexity

Medium

Less acidity, more body, some complexity

Medium-Dark

Second Crack (435–445°F [224–229°C])
Roast flavors appear
Little acidity, higher body, less complexity

Dark

Char burnt
Bitter, smoky

When the cell becomes heated up from roasting, some chemicals change from liquids to gases and some new gases are formed. These gases will take up more space than they did as liquids or solids, so they push against the cell walls, creating pressure, just like a pressure cooker. While the cell walls eventually break from the pressure (more on this later), the increased pressure conditions do help shape the roasting process.

"Science may never come up with a better office communication system than the coffee break."

— EARL WILSON —

— Did you know? —
While caffeine content might decrease somewhat as roasts get darker, the difference is so small that a daily coffee drinker's body would probably never notice the difference.

A great deal of research has been produced on green coffee chemistry and roasted coffee chemistry. Scientists have strived to identify the chemical reactions that occur during roasting as well as identify the compounds in green coffee and the resultant compounds that end up being created from the roasting process. To recount all that data here would be fairly meaningless and it would bore us all to tears. The truth is, while some groups of chemical reactions are known and lists of compounds exist, no nonscientific, practical use for the consumer or small business yet has come from any of it.

In short, we don't know much about what compounds in green coffee are important precursors for specific compounds in roasted coffee. Nor do we know what compounds in roasted coffee determine specific flavors for us. Yet, we know there are hundreds of compounds in the green and roasted beans, some of which might make it into our cups. We also know there are more than 1,000 volatile compounds in roasted coffee, less than 30 of which create the generic "coffee smell" experience, while others are recognizable as specific aromas when smelled on their own. Unfortunately, we don't know exactly what makes coffee taste acidy or sweet or floral or what tastes like chocolate and blueberry are connected to. When it comes to coffee taste chemistry, we're still in the dark ages.

These details aside, we know not only that roasting is important, but it is important how one roasts. At its simplest, coffee roasting is adding heat to coffee. However, how one applies heat (what kind of roaster is used) and when heat is applied throughout the roast have significant impacts on the final taste of the coffee. All modern roasters have at least one temperature probe inside the roasting chamber. This probe measures the air temperature at the location in which it is placed. When the chamber is filled and beans cover the probe, the temperature registered is an approximation of the bean's actual internal temperature. This temperature can help inform the person roasting of what should be adjusted during the roast and in future roasts. The manipulation of time and temperature during roasting is called roast profiling, which can be illustrated on a graph with a curve. The decision of what constitutes an acceptable roast profile is—or should be—taste, although length of the roast and bean color are valuable metrics as well.

The roast profile curve can be used to help a roaster manipulate the taste of a coffee. It can also be used to help us explore some basic coffee roast chemistry. When green coffee is first put into the roasting chamber, the temperature drops precipitously—the green beans are absorbing heat. Before too long, the temperature begins to stabilize and rise again. During this rise, chemical reactions begin to occur as evidenced by the evolution of novel compounds and a color change. Also, water is evaporated; coffee beans typically have a moisture content of 9 to12 percent and, by the end of the roast, have about 2 percent moisture. In addition, some of that water likely takes part in chemical reactions.

The slope at which the temperature rises is very important to coffee roasters. The slope is a measure of how fast the roast is progressing, with steeper slopes reflecting faster roasting during this roast phase. Controlling the speed of roasting also controls the speed of chemical reactions since it is a reflection of the amount of heat being added into the system. However, what this means chemically is unknown.

Once the bean color is decidedly light brown, the beans begin to crack or pop and undergo a size expansion. The cracking is the same phenomenon that happens to popcorn kernels as they transition from kernels to popcorn and is much like a balloon popping from being overfilled. Corn kernels pop because water, trapped inside, converts to steam. The steam creates pressure that eventually breaks the cells, giving us popped corn. The cracks in coffee are also caused by gases producing excess pressure and breaking out of the cells. Carbon dioxide is likely the major gas contributing to this jailbreak, and water is presumed to be fairly important.

Shortly after this crack, the roast could end and the coffee drunk. If left to continue, the bean color progresses through darker shades of brown and eventually into black. Somewhere between medium brown and very dark brown, the beans crack again. This, too, is the result of gases breaking more cells. Carbon dioxide is the main culprit here, but accomplices are certainly present.

Although we seem to know very little about roast chemistry, we actually know quite a lot. We really lack knowledge of coffee flavor chemistry and how the two connect. Current scientific instrumentation, computer power, and software are helping change this dearth of knowledge. Advances are coming, especially as more people become both coffee fiends and scientists. We just need to be patient!

— Did you know? —

Used coffee grounds can be used to generate biodiesel that can power cars, as a substrate to grow mushrooms, and even converted into a potable, though not necessarily tasty, alcohol!

ARE YOU AFRAID
★ ★ OF ★ ★
DARK ROASTS?

THE LITTLE COFFEE
KNOW-IT-ALL

STRONG. BOLD. DEEP. HEAVY. DARK. THESE ALL TEND TO MEAN ONE THING IN RELATION TO COFFEE: A DARK ROAST. THEY ARE PART OF OUR MODERN COFFEE LEXICON AND, OFTENTIMES, ARE SYNONYMOUS WITH GOURMET OR SPECIALTY COFFEE. YET, ALMOST EVERY COFFEE GEEK STAYS AS FAR AWAY FROM DARK-ROASTED COFFEES AS POSSIBLE. ARE THEY REALLY SO BAD WHEN SO MANY PEOPLE SEEM TO LIKE THEM? WE'LL COME BACK TO THIS.

We already know that roasting green coffee turns it into something we want to drink. We also know that how one roasts the coffee makes a difference. It shouldn't come as much of a surprise, then, that the final color of the coffee is relevant to our experience. The final color is really a function of the roast profile, and it is best thought of in that way. However, just referencing the roast color can be valuable as it often correlates to some bean characteristics and sensory experiences. Beware, though, sometimes, the roast profile can have an influence that beguiles the expectation of a particular roast level.

Coffee roasting is a function of temperature, as is cooking any food using heat. As the temperature of the bean increases and roasting progresses, some chemical reactions continue to occur while new ones come and go. The bean is continuously undergoing chemical changes. Thus, a lighter roast is chemically different than a darker roast; this is well researched by scientists and I'll spare you the gory details. The only general category of reactions worth mentioning is the Maillard reaction.

A Maillard reaction is one in which an amino acid (a component of protein) reacts with carbohydrates (often sugars). There isn't a specific end product from this reaction, especially as the reactions continue to occur; compounds formed from the reaction can react with each other, creating a dizzying array of complex molecules. Maillard reactions are common in cooking and are responsible for much of the browning we're familiar with. Think seared meat and the crust of bread. And of course, think brown in coffee. The brown compounds resulting from this reaction, called melanoidins, are significant in coffee: they can comprise some 25 percent of the solid material in a cup of coffee. They are also the likely source of any antioxidant behavior in coffee. While they likely contribute to the flavor of coffee in some way (no research exists on it), we can only guess at it in a roundabout way. Melanoidin content increases as roasts get darker (no surprise, there!). So, it isn't unfair to guess they may contribute to our sense of the difference between lighter and darker roasts.

Recent research on a compound called N-methylpyridinium (N-MP, a degradation product of trigonelline) is also worth

mentioning. It seems to be a significant inhibitor of gastric acid secretion in the stomach, potentially preventing nausea or indigestion—something that happens to some unfortunate coffee drinkers. As its occurrence is directly related to the destruction of trigonelline, its concentration in coffee increases as roasting progresses. In other words, darker roasted coffees may make for fewer upset stomachs.

For most of us, what we most want to understand about coffee roast levels is how they differ in taste. Coffee geeks have strong feelings about the roast levels they think are best and consumers are no different. However, to anyone wanting to try something new, a little guidance might be helpful. The literature repeatedly shows that as the roast level darkens, acidity, fruity/citrus, grassy/green/herbal, and aromatic intensity decrease. Concurrently, roasted, ashy/sooty, burnt/smoky, bitter, chemical/medicinal, burnt/acrid, sour, and pungent flavors all increase. That's a pretty grim picture but only because some of the research examined extreme roast cases. What must be realized is that these flavors occur on a continuum, with the intensity changing as the roast darkens.

Underroasted coffee is not very coffeelike. It tastes

leguminous, herby, and nutty. This taste happens just after first crack (see the section on coffee as a test tube) and lasts for a brief time. Once it is roasted just past that, all the coffee's soul is laid out for the palate. All the nuance, complexity, and acidity that could be in the taste exist at this point. Very light roasts are like puppies—full of verve and energy and spunk and sometimes just as annoying. As the roast progresses, those flavors might disappear or mature or become tempered. Coffee has many faces between very light roasts and approximately second crack. When the second crack happens, the process of roast begins to creep in. Thus, roasted, woody, smoky flavors begin to develop. From there, the process of roast becomes more and more dominate, approaching an end result of a black, charred bean that closely resembles charcoal.

There's no right answer for how light or how dark any given coffee should be roasted. Ultimately, the person roasting gets to decide, and she'll likely make that decision based on her personal belief of what best exemplifies the coffee in combination with what she thinks her market desires. Give the same coffee to ten roasters, and you'll get ten somewhat different coffees.

WHAT DO I CALL
= THIS =
ROAST LEVEL?

THE LITTLE COFFEE
KNOW-IT-ALL

AS WE FIND OURSELVES CARING MORE AND MORE ABOUT COFFEE, WE REALIZE THE ROAST LEVEL OF THE COFFEE IS IMPORTANT TO US. SO, WHEN WE GO TO BUY COFFEE, HOW DO WE TELL THE SELLER EXACTLY WHAT WE WANT? UNFORTUNATELY, IT IS A BIT MORE COMPLICATED THAN ANYONE FEELS IT SHOULD BE.

Simply using light, medium, and dark doesn't make sense because of the lack of agreement of what they mean; one person's medium is another person's light. Moreover, light can encompass quite a range of colors. Names like city, full city, French, and cinnamon are just as nondescript, as there's no standard for what color they actually correlate with. Terms like strong, bold, deep, and heavy are even more egregious, as they either refer to the concentration of the brew (strength) or could possibly refer to its viscosity.

Clever marketing brought us these terms and every coffee professional wishes these words would vanish from the roast level lexicon. Much to my dismay, I've never come across any terminology that works particularly well for describing roast levels.

Is there a more objective method that could be used? Yes. In fact, there are several, all of which are imperfect and all of which are distant and somewhat meaningless to the typical coffee drinker.

We can be referential to the

stages of roasting, and talk about roast level as the time before or after first or second crack. To an experienced roaster and especially to one familiar with a particular coffee (different coffees roast differently, as you'd expect), this is a fairly useful method of communicating roast level. However, as the length of the roast and events within the roast are, by definition, dependent on the roast profile, using the cracks as reference points are only useful if there is some knowledge of the profile.

Another method that is often used by scientists is weight loss. As the roast progresses, not only does the bean expand, nearly doubling in size by the end, but it loses a lot of moisture as it evaporates and solid matter is converted into volatile compounds that leave the bean. Very light roasts will lose around 12 percent of their weight while very dark roasts can lose as much as 30 percent of their weight. The minor drawback to this system is that weight loss depends on initial weight, which is heavily influenced by moisture content. While most green coffees tend to be in the 9 to 12 percent moisture range, not all of them are, and if not stored well, their moisture content can change. A coffee with a higher moisture content will have a greater

weight loss than one with a lower moisture content because more water (and the weight it added) will be driven off.

This is fairly minor problem for small roasters because even in the extreme case, the final weight loss between a high to low moisture content coffee will be pretty small. On the other hand, roasters who roast very large quantities of coffees or roast particularly dark may end the roast by quenching the coffee with a fine mist of water. While the expectation is that the water evaporates immediately, thereby cooling the coffee quickly, some water may remain and add weight back to the beans. In my opinion, the biggest problem with this as a tool is that training consumers to calibrate colors to weight loss may never be very successful; people just aren't used to thinking of weight and color as parallel ideas.

The last method that can be used to talk about roast color is the actual amount of lightness! More specifically, we can measure the amount of light reflected off the bean or grounds and assign an arbitrary number

to that particular amount of reflectance. This is already a common practice in the coffee industry, and the arbitrary numerical scale already exists. All one needs to make sense of it is a spectrophotometer, a machine that measures the reflectance or transmittance of a specific wavelength of light, and the coding that translates the number to a color. The latter part is simple, as one can create and even buy already-made colored discs that correspond to the numbers. The hard part is that spectrophotometers are expensive machines and usually only larger companies purchase them. Just as tricky is the consumer side of things, much like with weight loss, few consumers are going to learn which number corresponds to which roast level.

In the end, there is no perfect way of conveying roast level to someone else without showing them the bean. So, we'll just continue as we always have, using the tools we have on hand. Hopefully, someone will come up with something better someday.

WHAT DO YOU MEAN BY
★ ★ ★
COFFEE FRESHNESS?

THE LITTLE COFFEE
KNOW-IT-ALL

WE ALL WANT THE BEST POSSIBLE EXPERIENCE FROM OUR COFFEE. OBVIOUSLY, THIS MEANS IT OUGHT TO BE FRESH. THAT SOUNDS GOOD, OF COURSE, BUT WHAT EXACTLY DO WE MEAN BY FRESHNESS?

The implication is that at one point in time, coffee is fresh but it loses that freshness and becomes stale. Ultimately, we're talking about a taste in the coffee that changes from good to less good because it changes over time. Each coffee drinker probably has a different standard for what level of staleness is unacceptable. That standard is based on their past experience, their level of sensory acuity, and any number of things that might influence their sense of freshness. So, for a well-trained coffee geek, staling may be noticeable a week or two after roasting, while for a less discriminating consumer, it may be two to ten months before they notice (or care) about a change in the taste due to staling. Thus, there is no absolute definition, so we must discuss the issue with some generalities and wiggle room.

The next step is to consider freshness in light of coffee chemistry. We've established that roasting has an immense impact on coffee but it actually extends beyond the end of the actual roast. The bean not only passively changes but chemical reactions continue to occur. Some researchers have attempted to correlate these chemical changes to sensory response. While some insight has been gained, there are so many factors to account for that we only have a glimmer of the whole picture.

During roasting, many gases, or volatile compounds, are released or generated. The end of the roasting process doesn't mean the volatiles are no longer present. You know this intuitively because anytime you smell coffee, you smell a gas that's been released and is no longer in the bean. In the first twenty-four hours after roasting, the bulk of gases, composed mostly of carbon dioxide, are released from the bean. Over the course of several months, more and more volatiles escape from the bean structure, which is why coffee smells less intense over time. These volatiles that you smell are volatiles that you won't be drinking. Thus, the loss of these volatiles is a primary cause of staling. Since the volatiles are trapped in the bean and must diffuse out, the size of the bean particles play a significant role on their evolution. Smaller particles, with more surface area relative to their volume, offer much shorter distances for the volatiles to travel. If coffee is ground just after roasting, 26 to 59 percent of the carbon dioxide (and undoubtedly other volatiles) will be released immediately, with the larger value coming from smaller bean particle sizes that have a larger surface area to volume ratio.

The other primary cause of staling is the oxidation of compounds within the bean. While lipids (fats and oils) have been the main purview of coffee oxidation research, other molecules react as well and are surmised to play a role. Independent of the identification of specific oxidation reactions, the data demonstrate that coffee exposed to oxygen stales quicker than coffee not exposed to oxygen.

An indirect factor in coffee staling is ambient temperature. Higher temperatures increase the rate of chemical reactions. Thus, the warmer the room, the faster gas evolution and oxidation will occur. Also, higher levels of water activity (essentially, the amount of water available to participate in chemical reactions) hasten staling. In other words, exposure to humidity will allow coffee to absorb moisture, permitting bad things to happen. While many a coffee geek suggests light is detrimental to coffee freshness,

there is no evidence to support this in the literature. However, as some wavelengths of light contain enough energy to break chemical bonds (think UV and some plastics), it is reasonable to moot that light can play a damaging role.

Researchers working on coffee staling chemistry have identified a number of volatile compounds that either correlate with negative aromas or with negative aroma experiences. Unfortunately, there is no agreement on any one compound or even the ratio of two compounds that guarantees a successful measure of staleness. Part of the challenge is that the roast profile, roast level, and coffee origin all influence the volatile composition and thus makes finding definitive staling compound proxies difficult.

Interestingly, very few experiments that test the taste of coffee freshness (without any chemistry component) seem to exist. Some use untrained panelists (i.e, regular consumers) as their assessors while others use trained panelists to collect more refined data. As there are so few studies from which to draw conclusions, there isn't much of a story to tell. Moreover, each study had a very unique purpose; generating data to help populate this section of the book was not one of them. Thus, the next paragraph is going to

be a bit vague.

Average consumers, it seems, have a hard time telling the difference between coffees that are fresh or just a few weeks old, whether they were stored on the shelf or in the freezer. In other words, sometimes they can tell a difference and sometimes they cannot. This suggests that coffees that are less than a month from the roast date are probably perfectly acceptable to most consumers. On the other hand, with coffee far from the roast date (nine or eighteen months), a trained panel can easily describe differences between the coffees. Whether those differences are important (it was descriptive data, not performance) was not evaluated. A trained panel also seems to be able to identify coffees that were stored under different conditions or are of different ages starting around three weeks from the roast date (there was no statistical analyses in these reports, so it is difficult to be definitive here).

It is certainly evident that some people can identify the changes in coffee as it ages. Unfortunately, there is no one-size-fits-all answer as to what "stale" means in terms of days after roasting, nor do I think there ever will be one. Since the change in taste depends on sensory acuity and personal preference, the answer will always lie with the drinker.

HOW DO I KEEP
= MY =
COFFEE FRESH?

THE LITTLE COFFEE
KNOW-IT-ALL

YOU JUST PURCHASED A BAG OF COFFEE AND YOU NOTICE THAT JUST A LITTLE BIT ABOVE THE MIDWAY POINT OF THE BAG THERE IS A SMALL HOLE! IF YOU SQUEEZE THE BAG, YOU HEAR GAS ESCAPE THROUGH THE HOLE AND, HOPEFULLY, YOU SMELL SOMETHING WONDERFUL. WHY ON EARTH IS THERE A BELLY BUTTON ON THE BAG? YOU ALREADY KNOW THE SIMPLE ANSWER: TO LET OUT AIR. OF COURSE, IT IS MORE COMPLICATED THAN THAT. THAT HOLE IS PART OF A BIGGER DISCUSSION OF COFFEE FRESHNESS AND HOW BEST TO STORE ROASTED COFFEE TO MAINTAIN FRESHNESS.

Presumably, since we know the major factors that cause coffee to stale— gas evolution, high temperatures, oxidation, and humidity—we ought to able to control them to extend the shelf life of the coffee. By teasing some of the data available in the myriad of research on the topic, we can make some general statements that will help. However, without direct research to support our hypotheses, and the ones of the coffee industry at large, some of our conclusions will have to be educated guesses.

Let's address each staling factor individually, starting with gas evolution. Since smaller coffee pieces allow the release of more gas, keeping the coffee as intact as possible will help. Thus, grinding coffee ahead of time is a poor practice. Rather, grinding should occur just prior to brewing. The other potential way to slow down gas evolution (and all chemical reactions) is to decrease the storage temperature; cooler temperatures slow down chemical reactions and chemical mobility. Thus, storing coffee in the refrigerator or freezer will accomplish this. Unfortunately, I can't find any sensory data that explores specific taste changes when stored at cooler temperatures.

Coffee geeks abhor the idea, but, at best, they have some personal, anecdotal evidence to support it. Freezing coffee could run the risk of creating crystals that could shatter cells, much like grinding. Freezing could also lead to freezer burn, which probably isn't a flavor anyone wants to introduce to a coffee. Arguably, the biggest reason not to store coffee in the freezer is the risk of condensation forming on the beans as the beans come out of the freezer. This water may then lead to a deterioration of the quality by hastening the natural staling of coffee when the coffee is out of the freezer or by allowing ice crystals to form on the coffee if it is returned to the freezer. Refrigeration doesn't run the risk of crystal formation, but the condensation is still an issue. Ultimately, individual drinkers will have to decide this on their own, at least until some new research surfaces.

Preventing or minimizing oxidation reactions is as simple as keeping oxygen away from the roasted coffee beans. Of course, with the atmospheric concentration of oxygen at about 21 percent, that isn't so easy. Simply putting just-roasted coffee in an oxygen-impermeable container and sealing it doesn't solve the problem since still air trapped in the container is full of oxygen. Besides, even if coffee were sealed up in a container, the container would likely explode as a result of the pressure build-up from all the volatile compounds being released! So, either the air has to be completely sucked out of the container before it is sealed or all the air must be replaced with a gas that is completely inert, like nitrogen.

I have no knowledge that any company packages just-roasted coffee and then evacuates the air before sealing it, though it seems like a worthwhile strategy. Many larger roasters do flush bags with nitrogen before sealing them. Some research supports this as an effective means of extending the acceptability of the coffee farther from the roast date than by using normal air.

Lastly, controlling the amount of water coffee is exposed to is fairly simple. If the coffee is packed in an oxygen-impermeable container, then the container is also likely to be water impermeable. After the container in opened, keeping the coffee in an air-tight container that is waterproof should help minimize exposure to any humidity in the air, although, if the air was full of moisture when the coffee was sealed or closed in a container, then the container won't offer any protection.

So, what's the story with the bag and its belly button? The bags that have them are made out of oxygen-impermeable materials. Generally, they prevent many gases from passing through. Thus, as mentioned before, if freshly roasted coffee is sealed in a bag, it is liable to explode. The belly button, more formally known as a one-way valve, is a crafty device that allows gas to exit the bag but prevents any gas from entering. It is a release valve; the carbon dioxide and other volatile compounds can escape but oxygen cannot enter.

The one-way valve is a fantastic tool but it has its limitations. For one thing, unless the air trapped in the bag while sealing it is replaced with something inert, preventing oxygen from entering is irrelevant; the bag is already full of it (though the valve still prevents the bag from exploding). Secondly, once the bag is opened by the consumer, any internal protection is lost and the consumer must repackage the coffee as best as possible.

Ultimately, we aren't able to prevent the staling process from occurring. At best, it can be delayed. However, if coffee is drunk within a few weeks of roasting, the need to delay staling is most likely unnecessary. After all, the freshly roasted coffee will still be pretty fresh!

HOW IS COFFEE
★ ★ ★
DECAFFEINATED?

MORE THAN A FEW PEOPLE OUT THERE CAN'T FUNCTION WITHOUT A CUP OF COFFEE A DAY, IF NOT TWO OR THREE CUPS. MOST COFFEE DRINKERS NOT ONLY RELY ON THE CAFFEINE IN COFFEE BUT THEY RELISH THE ENERGY AND AWARENESS IT BRINGS. HOWEVER, THERE'S A DEDICATED GROUP OF DRINKERS WHO EITHER DON'T WANT THE CAFFEINE OR PHYSICALLY CAN'T TOLERATE IT. SO, THEY DRINK COFFEE FROM WHICH THE CAFFEINE HAS BEEN REMOVED.

As of now, there are no arabica varieties in cultivation with caffeine content that meets international standards for what constitutes decaffeinated coffee. Thus, all decaf coffee comes from manually removing it from ordinary coffee. There are four commonly used solvents for doing this: methylene chloride, ethyl acetate, carbon dioxide, and water.

No matter which solvent is used, the beginning of the process is the same. Green coffee beans are steamed or soaked in water to make the caffeine more available to the solvents and to make it easier for the solvents to penetrate the beans. From here, two main pathways exist: direct solvent extraction or indirect extraction.

In direct extraction, where methylene chloride and ethyl

acetate are used, the wet green beans are treated directly with the solvent for some eight to twelve hours. Then, the solvent is removed and the beans are steamed (to help drive off any remaining solvent) and dried before roasting. Unfortunately, these solvents don't extract just caffeine. Thus, other compounds, which may be related to quality, may also be extracted. This is one reason why decaf has a historically bad reputation for quality (the other reason is that low quality coffees were often used: junk in, junk out).

Carbon dioxide is a terrible solvent for caffeine under normal conditions as the solubility of caffeine in it is low. This is not surprising, as carbon dioxide is a gas at room temperature! However, if carbon dioxide is taken to its supercritical state—where it has liquid and gaslike properties simultaneously—it improves, and if a bit of water is added, it becomes much better. To take carbon dioxide to its supercritical point requires special equipment to significantly increase temperature and pressure. The great thing is that supercritical carbon dioxide seems to selectively extract caffeine and not much else.

The indirect method allows for water to be the only solvent in direct contact with the beans. Water can be used to extract the caffeine and other compounds and then the water solution is treated with a solvent or passed through a filter to remove the caffeine, pulling it away from the beans. The other compounds can then be returned to the coffee beans before drying them down.

When water is the only solvent used, a clever trick is employed to prevent compounds

other than caffeine from being removed. The process begins with soaking the wet green beans with water and then removing the caffeine from the solution, as in the indirect method. Then, the beans are discarded! The solution, sans caffeine but with the other stuff, is then the solvent used to extract the caffeine from the next batch of coffee. Doing it this way means very little noncaffeine material is extracted by the solvent. Now, nothing has to be returned to the coffee and it is believed that the end result tastes better.

There will always be a place for decaf coffee, as there will always be someone who loves the taste of the coffee

> "I was taken by the power that savoring a simple cup of coffee can have to connect people and create community."
>
> — HOWARD SCHULTZ —

at all hours of the day but doesn't want to deal with the physiological effects of the caffeine. Modern decaffeinated coffees can have excellent quality. Like all technology, the methods for removing caffeine are continuously improving. Thus, expect the quality to improve even more.

WILL A DARK ROAST
= KEEP ME =
UP AT NIGHT?

THE LITTLE COFFEE
KNOW-IT-ALL

IT IS HARD TO NOT LOVE COFFEE FOR ITS CAFFEINE CONTENT. SURE, IT TASTES GREAT, BUT LIFE SEEMS SO MUCH MORE DELIGHTFUL WITH AN EXTRA LIFT IN YOUR STEP! YET, SOMETIMES, YOU WANT THE CAFFEINE BUT MAYBE A LITTLE BIT LESS THAN USUAL. SO, DECAF IS OUT OF THE QUESTION. IS THE SOLUTION TO DRINK A DARKER ROASTED COFFEE? DO DARKER ROASTS HAVE LESS CAFFEINE?

The answer, unfortunately, is not clear. The available data are all over the place. Some research shows that the concentration of caffeine increases with darker roasts while other research shows that it decreases. Some research even shows no changes at all! What are we to make of all this—how can we see completely opposite patterns with something that seems so cut and dry? If we consider what we know about roasting and add to it some details of how caffeine behaves in the universe, we might be able to guess at the answers.

As coffee is roasted longer and darker, it loses mass: gaseous molecules are created during roasting and they leave the bean. Longer roast times produce more gases, which mean lower weights. Some molecules in the beans, however, don't change at all during roasting. Consequently, as roast levels darken, these static compounds increase in concentration. We can demonstrate this with an example using mythical compound q. Let's say the concentration of q in the unroasted bean was 5 parts q to 100 parts bean. In a light roast, some of the bean vaporizes leaving only 85 parts bean but q stays the same. So, now the concentration is 5 q/85 bean. If the roast darkens a lot, the bean may only have 75 parts left, making q much more concentrated merely because it could tolerate the heat!

This behavior would certainly help explain how the concentration of caffeine increases in darker roasts. If the actual content remains constant while lots of stuff around it is leaving. If this were always the case, then we'd always see an increase in caffeine concentration with darker roasts. But, that's not what we find.

Caffeine seems to be a fairly stable molecule in coffee. In other words, it doesn't seem to combine or interact with other molecules, though there isn't any research exploring whether this is true or not. However, it does have a quirky trait whereby it tends to not obey the typical transition steps between phase changes. So, instead of changing from a

solid to a liquid to a gas, it often skips the liquid phase and turns directly into a gas, a process called sublimation. Sublimation for caffeine can begin at 178°C (352°F). While it is very difficult to measure the actual internal bean temperature during roasting, it is simple to measure the temperature of the mass of beans, which is probably near the temperature inside a bean. As most roasts easily exceed bean mass temperatures of 215°C (419°F) and can go as high as 235°C (455°F), it is perfectly reasonable to suspect that some caffeine in the bean sublimates and drifts away from the bean.

If this happens, then it explains the caffeine decrease seen in dark roasts. In fact, some research does indeed show that total caffeine content decreases with darker roasts.

What about the data that demonstrated no change in caffeine concentration in either direction? Well, it is possible that both of those phenomena occurred simultaneously at just the right levels as to maintain a constant caffeine concentration. I don't think it is that

straightforward, though. There are several reports where beans were processed differently or were of different quality grades and their caffeine contents were different. This suggests that some kind of interaction between caffeine and biological and/or chemical processes exists. The effect of this interaction may be the unpredictability of how caffeine behaves during the roasting process.

At the end of the day, all this discussion of how the caffeine concentration is changing is probably moot. In all cases, the changes in concentration are pretty small, amounting to 0.1 percent or less of a difference from the lightest to the darkest roast. Thus, in a practical, everyday, I-want-to-enjoy-coffee basis, the amount of caffeine in a cup produced from a very light roast compared to that of a cup produced from a very dark roast is pretty small. It is so small, in fact, that a person who drinks a cup of coffee a day would probably experience no physiological difference between the two cups based upon their caffeine content!

Did you know?

Although Hawaii is the only U.S. state that produces significant amounts of coffee, there is a small farm in California that grows some coffee.

WHAT'S THE DEAL
WITH ACRYLAMIDE?

AS WE KNOW, THE MAILLARD REACTION IS RESPONSIBLE FOR THE PRODUCTION OF A VAST ARRAY OF MOLECULES. ONE OF THEM, ACRYLAMIDE, A PRODUCT FROM THE REACTION OF THE AMINO ACID ASPARAGINE AND SUGARS, HAS RECEIVED AN AWFUL LOT OF ATTENTION SINCE 2002. WHILE HARMLESS IN THE ENVIRONMENT, SOME STUDIES HAVE SHOWN IT TO CAUSE CANCER IN RATS AND, IN SITUATIONS WITH HIGH ENOUGH EXPOSURE (TYPICALLY FROM AN OCCUPATIONAL SCENARIO), TO BE A NEUROTOXIN TO HUMANS. MANY OTHER STUDIES HAVE SHOWN IT TO BE PREVALENT IN A BUNCH OF FOOD PRODUCTS THAT WE COOK AND EAT QUITE REGULARLY, LIKE BREAD, POTATOES (ESPECIALLY FRIED ONES), AND OF COURSE, COFFEE. ONCE ESTABLISHED THAT ACRYLAMIDE WAS PRESENT IN SOME COMMONLY CONSUMED FOODS, WORRY SPREAD QUICKLY ON A GLOBAL SCALE. WHILE THE MEDIA DOESN'T FOCUS ON IT AS MUCH AS IT ONCE DID, RESEARCHERS AND COMPANIES ARE STILL TRYING TO FIGURE OUT IF IT IS REALLY A PROBLEM AND, JUST IN CASE IT IS, HOW TO DEAL WITH IT. AFTER ALL, NOBODY WANTS TO GIVE UP POTATO CHIPS AND COFFEE!

Lighter roasted coffees have the highest amount of acrylamide, potentially halving almost seven times as much as dark roasted coffees.

Acrylamide occurs in pretty small concentrations in foods; it is usually measured in parts per billion. In roasted coffee, an average amount is 253 ppb. In a coffee beverage, the concentration is higher. In espresso, for example, the concentration can average around 40 parts per million. In nonpressurized brewing methods (like a full immersion or drip coffee), the average is about one-quarter of that. Acrylamide is very soluble in water (2.04 kg/L [20.44 lbs/gal]) and all of it can be extracted from the coffee grounds if enough water or contact time is available.

Due to its higher asparagine content, roasted *C. canephora* can have almost twice as much acrylamide as *C. arabica*. Other differences in concentration occur due to roast level and storage time. While formation of acrylamide requires a certain amount of heat, too much will destroy it. Thus, lighter roasted coffees have the highest amount of acrylamide, potentially having almost seven times as much as dark roasted coffees. It also appears that the longer roasted coffee is stored, the less acrylamide can be extracted into the brew. Whether it decomposes or irreversibly binds to the coffee matrix is not known.

Unfortunately, it is not clear whether acrylamide is carcinogenic to humans. Most epidemiological research suggests that it is not, but a small handful suggests otherwise. Therefore, coming up with a clear risk assessment has proven difficult. Various food industry groups have developed strategies to help reduce the content of acrylamide in their products, but aside from sticking to arabica coffee and dark roasts, the coffee industry has been unable to develop any technology or technique to reduce the acrylamide content without impinging on the quality of the coffee.

Although coffee can supply a significant proportion of the dietary acrylamide consumption (5.5 percent to 39 percent), the fear of coffee being carcinogenic is practically nonexistent. A great deal of research has attempted to link coffee consumption and cancer, but no connections have yet been made across a wide variety of cancer types. If coffee cannot be linked to cancer, then acrylamide consumption from coffee cannot be threatening. Unfortunately, we cannot know whether acrylamide itself simply isn't harmful to us, or whether coffee contains other compounds that protect us from the dangers of acrylamide. In either case, it seems we don't have much to worry about while drinking our morning brew.

IS THERE MORE TO KNOW
= IF I'M A =
HOME ROASTER

THE LITTLE COFFEE
KNOW-IT-ALL

ROASTING ISN'T ROCKET SCIENCE. IT IS MUCH, MUCH EASIER. IN FACT, IT IS SO EASY THAT ANYONE CAN DO IT, EVEN AT HOME. WHILE HOME ROASTING IS VERY SIMILAR TO WHAT TRANSPIRES IN A COMMERCIAL ROASTERY, THERE ARE A FEW EXTRA TIDBITS THAT MAY BE HANDY TO KNOW IF YOU INTEND TO TAKE YOUR COFFEE HABIT TO THE NEXT LEVEL. BOTH INVOLVE THE TWO ESSENTIAL ITEMS YOU NEED TO MAKE IT HAPPEN: GREEN COFFEE AND A ROASTER.

Acquiring green coffee is pretty easy these days. If you were to walk into a roastery and ask them to sell you small amounts of green coffee, they most likely would do so. There are also a number of different online retailers that will sell you green coffee for home roasting.

What really matters with green coffee is storage. While it can be a stable product, with the ability to last relatively unchanged for well over a year after harvesting, it must be stored properly. Basically, this means green coffee must be kept dry and at a cozy temperature. If the humidity is high, the coffee will absorb moisture. If it absorbs enough moisture, microorganisms may start chomping on it and growing, running the risk of ruining the coffee. Higher moisture contents may also facilitate natural degradation of the green bean, as will storing the coffee at temperatures that are too warm.

When green coffee doesn't age well and it isn't caused by mold, it develops a flavor known in the industry as "baggy". It got this name because for most of recent coffee history, green coffee has been stored in jute bags and the baggy flavor tends to be woody/cardboard/grassy, not so unlike the way we imagine jute might taste.

Fortunately, storing small amounts of green coffee

properly in your home is simple. If the climate in your home is controlled throughout the year to make you comfortable (i.e., you use air conditioning and heating), then the coffee will likely stay fresh for many months, even for more than a year, assuming you don't store it, say, next to the shower. If the conditions aren't that controlled, then merely keeping the coffee in airtight containers (plastic, glass, or metal) will also do the trick. There's also anecdotal evidence that storing coffee in the freezer is an excellent way of preserving it with no known side effects (while crystal formation doesn't seem to be a problem, the same risks that apply to storing roasted coffee in the freezer would apply to green coffee, as well).

Once you've got the green bean storage situation figured out, all you need is something with which to roast them! As a home roaster, you will be constrained by the tools available, thus, don't expect to be manipulating the roast profile too much; home roasting machines aren't as sophisticated as commercial machines. This isn't to say you can't create an excellent coffee at home, just that you may not get to explore the finer points of roasting too much.

You can roast coffee with pretty much any tool you have that will transfer heat to the coffee. Most people start roasting coffee at home the way it is typically done in Ethiopia—on a skillet or other heated pan. This works, but roasting the beans evenly is very tricky, even with constant stirring. Other people start with hot air popcorn poppers. They hold only a small amount of coffee but hot air is a very efficient way of transferring heat to coffee. Commercial air roasters do exist, but they are much less popular than drum roasters, which are just large, metal cylinders that are heated externally and transfer the heat through the drum.

If home roasting becomes a bigger part of your life, you can purchase an actual home roaster. There are several different types available, each with its own pros and cons. Both air and drum roasters are manufactured. Of course, if you like to work with your hands, you can always just build your own home roaster!

PART THREE
THE BREW

**THE LITTLE COFFEE
KNOW-IT-ALL**

DOES COFFEE HAVE

★ ★ ★

ANYTHING TO DO WITH

CHEMISTRY

THE LITTLE COFFEE
KNOW-IT-ALL

WE OFTEN THINK CHEMISTRY IS MADE UP OF EXPLOSIONS AND COLOR CHANGING LIQUIDS AND THOSE INCREDIBLY HARD TO PRONOUNCE CHEMICAL NAMES FOUND ON FOOD INGREDIENT LABELS. WELL, CHEMISTRY IS ALL THOSE THINGS AND SO MUCH MORE. CHEMISTRY IS ABOUT THE INTERACTIONS OF ATOMS AND MOLECULES, WHICH MEANS IT HAS TO DO WITH A GOOD DEAL OF THINGS WE SEE AND TOUCH AND EAT EVERY DAY. CHEMISTRY HAPPENS ALL AROUND US ALL THE TIME. MAKING COFFEE IS CHEMISTRY.

The basic brewing parameters are all just basic chemistry. If we can master a few of those, then making coffee loses its reputation of being like rocket science and it just becomes making coffee. Coffee brewing is nothing more than the simple extraction of solutes (coffee solids) with a solvent (water) from a matrix (coffee grounds) to produce a solution (coffee beverage). Any parameter that influences the extraction is something we need to know about: energy (temperature), water quality, surface area, contact time,

agitation, pressure, brew ratio, filter type, and container type.

By manipulating all of these parameters and balancing their effects relative to each other, we're able to make an array of different coffee brewers, each producing a slightly different brew.

In the next nine sections, we will explore each of these parameters to understand the underlying chemistry and physics that explain how each parameter functions. We'll also draw upon the scientific literature to find out how changing each parameter

might change the taste of a cup of coffee. In the end, this knowledge won't help us design the perfect coffee brewer. Rather, it will help us understand how brewing works, so that we can effectively brew yummy coffee with whatever tools we're given.

★ ★ ★

BREWING PARAMETER

ENERGY
(TEMPERATURE)

NOTHING REALLY HAPPENS IN THE UNIVERSE WITHOUT ENERGY. IF YOU CAN TAKE ENOUGH OF IT AWAY, EVERYTHING STOPS. WATCH AN ATOM AT A TEMPERATURE OF ABSOLUTE ZERO KELVIN (-459.67°F/-273.15°C) AND IT WILL BE COMPLETELY STILL (OR SO THE THEORY GOES). ADD ENERGY BACK TO THAT ATOM AND IT BEGINS TO VIBRATE. AS MORE AND MORE ENERGY IS APPLIED, IT MOVES AROUND MORE. HENCE, A SOLID TURNS INTO A LIQUID (MELTS) BEFORE TURNING INTO A GAS (EVAPORATES). A CONSEQUENCE OF THE ENERGY IS THAT THE VIBRATION CAN TURN INTO ACTUAL MOVEMENT.

★ ★ ★

"Once you wake up and smell the coffee, it's hard to go back to sleep."

— FRAN DRESCHER —

One very common form of energy we're familiar with is heat (light and sound are other familiar forms). The hotter an object is, the more energy it has. Thus, the hotter it is, the more vibration or movement its atoms or molecules have. Another thing about heat is that it transfers energy from molecules that have an excess of it to molecules that have less of it.

This applies to coffee brewing in two ways. First, the heat contained in the brewing water has a big influence on the extraction. Hotter water with its higher energy and dancing molecules can extract more coffee solids, faster, than colder water because the energy facilitates molecular movement (coffee solids) into the water. Not only does it happen faster, but more molecules will move into the water (hot things can dissolve more molecules than cold things; this is why we heat water to make simple syrup). Second, heat from the water transfers to the grounds, filter, container, and air around it, resulting in brewing water that is instantly colder than was intended and a final brew that is colder than the water that went into it.

The temperature of the water used to brew coffee, then, is very important to the molecular content of the brew and our organoleptic experience of it. If the temperature is low, the coffee can taste thin (low body/viscosity), flat, and have a low flavor intensity. As the temperature increases, the bitterness, acidity, astringency, roastiness, acridness, body, and flavor intensities increase. The question remains, what is the temperature where all these flavors balance in such a way that we think they all taste good?

Ultimately, that decision is made by the drinker. However, we have an idea of what most people like, all things being equal. The brew temperature should be 90–96°C (194–205°F). While this can be somewhat pieced together using articles in the scientific literature, we know this because back in the 1950s, Dr. Earl E. Lockhart did an enormous amount of research to figure out just what temperature of water brewed up coffee that most people liked.

Ultimately, the temperature ideal for brewing coffee is up to the drinker, but more than a half century of research has determined that most people prefer coffee that's been brewed between 194-205°F (90-96°C).

★ ★ ★

BREWING PARAMETER
WATER QUALITY

EXTRACTION OCCURS BECAUSE THE SOLUTES CREATE A MORE ENERGETICALLY STABLE SITUATION IN THE SOLVENT, RATHER THAN IN THE MATRIX. IN ADDITION, OTHER CONDITIONS CAN INFLUENCE THE EXTRACTION (LIKE TEMPERATURE AND PRESSURE). THE ENERGETICALLY STABLE SITUATION IS DEPENDENT ON THE COMPOSITION OF THE SOLVENT ITSELF, IMPURITIES IN THE SOLVENT, AND THE AMOUNT OF SOLUTE ALREADY IN THE SOLVENT.

In other words, not every solvent is going to extract every solute because they are chemically different. Think oil and water. It is very hard to extract oil from a matrix if you're using pure water. A concentration gradient is also required so that the solute in the matrix will diffuse to the solution. A concentration gradient exists if in one location there is a high concentration of a particle and in a nearby location there is a lower concentration of the particle. Particles tend to move down the gradient, from high to low concentration, until the gradient ceases to exist and the concentration is the same everywhere (the particles never actually stop moving in any direction, rather, they just fill up the space they're in and are spread across it evenly). Thus, if the solvent is already saturated

Characteristic	Target	Acceptable Range
Odor	Clean/Fresh, Odor free	
Color	Clear color	
Total chlorine	O mg/L	
TDS	150 mg/L	75–250 mg/L
Calcium hardness	4 grains or 68 mg/L	1–5 grains or 17 mg/L–85 mg/L
Total alkalinity	40 mg/L	at or near 40 mg/L
pH	7.0	6.5–7.5
Sodium	10 mg/L	at or near 10 mg/L

with solute, additional solute will not be removed from the matrix.

The coffee matrix is very complex and the molecules we hope to extract come in all sorts of shapes, sizes, and electrical charge densities. Water is a great solvent (especially hot water) because it has the capacity to hold on to (dissolve) all kinds of molecules. Pure water (completely distilled, with nothing else dissolved in it) will extract coffee solids differently than water with impurities (ions, metals, other molecules—basically things that make water hard, soft, or distasteful). This is because the impurities influence the concentration gradients or alter the electrical conductivity of the water. In short, not all water is equal!

The first rule of thumb about using water for your coffee is that if it tastes good as plain water, it might be good for coffee. Unfortunately, that isn't always a guarantee. If you think water is a problem for you, procure filtered water or get a filter system that moderates the contents of the water. You can always check with your municipality's water provider for a report on the quality. This chart, supplied by the Specialty Coffee Association of America, is a recommended guide to water quality for brewing coffee. Recent research suggests an additional recommendation: brewing water should have 1 part bicarbonate (HCO_3) to 1—2 parts double-charged cations (Ca^{2+} and Mg^{2+}).

"We want to do a lot of stuff; we're not in great shape. We didn't get a good night's sleep. We're a little depressed. Coffee solves all these problems in one delightful little cup."

— JERRY SEINFELD —

★ ★ ★

BREWING PARAMETER

SURFACE AREA

"If during their efforts coffee tasters find something in the taste that resists being said, that perhaps even resists being organized into their discourse, that is where they focus their attention."

— KENNETH LIBERMAN —

IMAGINE YOU HAD A WEDDING CAKE IN FRONT OF YOU AND YOU WANTED TO HAVE A BITE FROM THE VERY MIDDLE AND YOU COULD ONLY USE A FORK TO GET TO IT. NOW, IMAGINE THE CAKE WAS SLICED AND SEPARATED AND YOU WANTED TO HAVE A BITE FROM THE VERY CENTER OF EACH SLICE, USING ONLY A FORK. WHICH ONE WOULD BE EASIER TO ACCOMPLISH? EATING A BIT OF EACH INDIVIDUAL SLICE! THE REASON IS THAT THE AMOUNT OF SURFACE AREA RELATIVE TO THE VOLUME OF EACH INDIVIDUAL PIECE IS MUCH LARGER THAN THE SURFACE AREA RELATIVE TO THE VOLUME OF THE WHOLE CAKE. THUS, THERE IS LESS DISTANCE REQUIRED TO GET FROM ANY POINT ON THE OUTSIDE OF A SLICE TO ITS CENTER THAN THERE IS WITH THE ENTIRE CAKE.

The same is true with a particle of coffee. A whole bean of coffee has much smaller surface area-to-volume ratio than a ground-up bean. Thus, getting to the middle of an individual unit is easier with ground coffee. Now, exchange water for the fork in our example and the importance of grinding becomes apparent. In short, the smaller the particle size, the higher the number of solutes that will be extracted from the matrix.

If the main goal of brewing coffee is to achieve a high-quality cup, then any person brewing should strive for a uniform extraction of solutes from the grounds. To do this, each coffee unit should have the same surface area to volume ratio, that is, they should be the same size. If they aren't, the bigger pieces will release fewer solutes than the smaller pieces. The pieces should be the same shape, too. Pieces of various shapes will interact with the water molecules differently, causing each unit to release inconsistent amounts of solutes during extraction.

Determining the correct grind size for brewing is not simple. The grind size interacts with other variables we're exploring here and, ultimately, all the parameters must be balanced to create the desired beverage. All other things being equal, the grind size does play its own role in the taste of the final beverage. In general, finer grinds can produce less acidity (though some will suggest increased sourness), more bitterness, and more body than coarser grinds.

For the best brew possible, your grounds should be as uniformly sized and shaped as possible. It will mean more consistency in how each piece interacts with the water molecules.

★ ★ ★

BREWING PARAMETER

AGITATION

MOST PEOPLE RECOGNIZE THAT IF YOU ARE TRYING TO DISSOLVE SALT INTO A LIQUID, IT OCCURS MUCH MORE QUICKLY IF YOU STIR IT. THE SAME IS TRUE FOR EXTRACTING SOLIDS FROM A MATRIX. AGITATION MOVES THINGS ALONG. THIS IS TRUE BECAUSE AGITATION CREATES OPPORTUNITIES FOR MOLECULES TO BECOME BUDDIES.

Dissolution and extraction work because the solute molecules are attracted to the solvent molecules. The solute molecules then leave their place of origin to go hang out somewhere in the solvent. Think of a grain of salt, which is composed of many molecules of salt, as being a group of men in a room waiting to enter a dance hall. They aren't allowed to go into the dance hall until a dance partner (a solvent molecule) comes to get them. If the dance partners walk up to the room to get a man, the room will empty at a certain rate. If the dance partners run to the room to grab a man, then the room will empty out at a faster rate. Thus, anything that speeds up the movement of the dance

partners will speed up clearing out the room.

As discussed in the energy section, increasing the amount of energy in a molecule speeds up its movement. Thus, increasing the temperature of a solvent increases the rate of dissolution or extraction. Alternatively, manually agitating the entire system will also speed up the movement of the solvent and hasten the dissolution or extraction. Simply, agitation increases the number of encounters between the solute and the solvent.

When brewing coffee, this principle is manipulated least amongst all other parameters. Rarely do brewers intentionally agitate a brewing system to

speed things up. That said, most brew methods have a certain amount of agitation in them. For example, when water is dropped on a bed of coffee grounds, it trickles down through the grounds because of gravity. So, while the person brewing isn't actively speeding up the brewing time by agitating the system, there is agitation occurring.

★ ★ ★
BREWING PARAMETER
PRESSURE

EVERYTHING BEHAVES DIFFERENTLY UNDER PRESSURE, EVEN PEOPLE. WHEN IT COMES TO EXTRACTION, INCREASING THE PRESSURE NOT ONLY SPEEDS THINGS UP, BUT IT TENDS TO EXTRACT MORE SOLUTES THAN WOULD OTHERWISE BE REMOVED WITHOUT THE PRESSURE. INTERESTINGLY, GASES IN PARTICULAR, BEHAVE VERY DIFFERENTLY.

Imagine a small group of kids hanging out in a hallway. If a few other kids come walking down the hallway, some bumping into each other may occur but, generally, the stationary kids aren't going to be touched and they aren't going to go anywhere. If a large group of kids comes pouring down the hallway, nearly everybody is going to be bumped and some of them will get dragged down the hall with the flow. In this analogy, the kids just milling about are solutes and the other group coming down the hall is the solvent. In the first case, the solvent is not under pressure and in the second case it is. In the high-pressure scenario, the force of the solvent is so high that it is going to extract solutes faster and it is likely to snag solutes that wouldn't likely be dislodged.

When gas is under pressure, it becomes much more soluble in liquid. So, for a given volume of liquid, you can put more gas into it when it is pressurized. Of course, when the pressure is released, the gas leaves the liquid. This is what happens with carbonated beverages. They are saturated with gas and sealed under pressure. When the container is opened, the gas leaves the liquid as bubbles, creating the carbonation that we so enjoy.

The most familiar coffee brew method that uses elevated pressure is espresso. The pressurized water (approximately nine times the pressure of air at sea level) is forced through a bed of coffee, yanking out a greater amount of solutes than would emerge without the pressure. The water also picks up a great deal of gas from the coffee. When the brew leaves the bed of coffee, the gas is released. However, whereas with carbonated beverages the gas escapes to the air, oils extracted from the coffee capture the gas, creating bubbles. We call these bubbles "crema!"

— Did you know? —

Milk curdles in coffee because the coffee's pH is low enough to denature and precipitate the proteins in the milk.

An espresso machine is the most common example of a brewing method that uses elevated pressure. The water it's forcing through the grounds is approximately nine times the pressure of air at sea level.

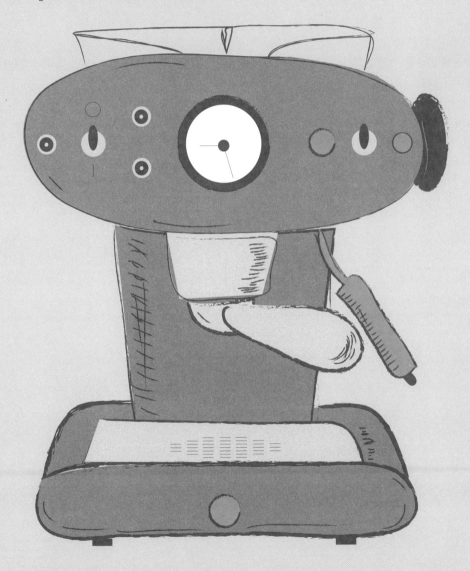

★ ★ ★

BREWING PARAMETER
BREW RATIO

THE SECRET TO STRONG COFFEE IS NOT TO ROAST IT DARKER, IT IS JUST ADDING MORE COFFEE! PERHAPS THE EASIEST OF BREWING PARAMETERS TO UNDERSTAND IS THE BREW RATIO, THAT IS, THE RATIO OF WATER TO COFFEE USED TO BREW THE BEVERAGE.

— Did you know? —

According to legend, coffee was discovered by a goat herder named Khaldi.

MIT chemistry professor E.E. Lockhart studied coffee preferences in the 1950s and determined that most people preferred a water-to-coffee ratio of about 18:1. In other words, weigh your water, divide by 18, and use that much ground coffee when you brew.

Simply, if there is more matrix to extract from, then the solvent is likely to extract a larger number of solutes. Most people understand this implicitly: if the ratio is lower (less water, more coffee), the coffee is stronger, whereas higher ratios (more water, less coffee) produce brews that are weaker.

Like all aspects of coffee quality, there is no one true brew ratio. If we return to Dr. Lockhart's work, he found that most people preferred a water to coffee ratio of about 18:1. However, that means people also had preferences with higher and lower ratios. Generally, when decreasing the ratio, the taste of the resultant brew becomes increasingly burnt/smoky, more fruity/citrus, more acid, more salty, more astringent, and its body (viscosity) increases. In other words, most flavors become more intense.

Water

17.42:1

"The Golden Ratio"

Coffee

★ ★ ★

BREWING PARAMETER
CONTACT TIME

ANOTHER BREWING PRINCIPLE THAT IS EASY TO UNDERSTAND IS CONTACT TIME, THAT IS, THE AMOUNT OF TIME THE SOLVENT AND MATRIX ARE IN CONTACT WITH EACH OTHER. MORE CONTACT TIME PRODUCES GREATER EXTRACTION OF SOLUTES. THIS HAPPENS BECAUSE THE SOLVENT MOLECULES CAN EITHER INTERACT WITH MORE SITES ON THE MATRIX OR SOLVENT MOLECULES THAT OTHERWISE WOULD NOT INTERACT WITH THE MATRIX ARE MORE LIKELY TO FINALLY DO SO. THERE IS A POINT OF DIMINISHING RETURNS WHERE NO ADDITIONAL CONTACT TIME WILL PRODUCE ADDITIONAL EXTRACTION; AT SOME POINT, EVERYTHING THAT CAN BE EXTRACTED WILL BE EXTRACTED AND NO EXTRA TIME WILL CHANGE THAT.

If you hold all the other parameters constant and just adjust the contact time, the taste of the beverage will change. With longer contact times, intensity of body, coffee flavor, bitterness, and sourness all increase. With contact times that are too short, many organoleptic traits have very low intensities, not always dissimilar from brewing a coffee with a large water-to-coffee ratio.

★ ★ ★

BREWING PARAMETER

FILTER TYPE

IN MOST MODERN COFFEE SOCIETIES, IT IS STANDARD PRACTICE TO FILTER THE COFFEE GROUNDS FROM THE LIQUID. AFTER ALL, WHO WANTS A MOUTH FULL OF WET GROUNDS WHEN TRYING TO DRINK COFFEE? FILTERS CAN BE MADE FROM ALL SORTS OF MATERIALS—METAL, PAPER, NYLON, OR COTTON, JUST TO NAME A FEW. WHILE THE FILTER TYPE DOESN'T INFLUENCE THE EXTRACTION OF THE MATRIX, IT DOES HAVE THE POTENTIAL TO INFLUENCE THE TASTE OF THE BEVERAGE.

Filter types are typically dividend into two groups: metal and nonmetal. The reason for this is that metal filters are just screens with tiny holes in them, whether they are gold or stainless steel filters used in gravity-fed brewers, mesh filters used in full immersion devices (e.g., a press pot), or portafilters used in espresso machines. Therefore, anything small enough to fit through the hole, be it a very small coffee particle or a solute, will fit through the hole. Consequently, coffees brewed with metal filters always have some amount of fine particulate and solutes, whereas those brewed with nonmetal filters typically don't. We know that metal filters permit more oils through to the brew than nonmetal filters (other molecular types have not been much explored). These coffees have more intense bodies and somewhat different flavors than those made with nonmetal filters. Metal filters typically do not impart a metallic taste on the brew, as they are often made of inert metals.

Nonmetal filters, whether they are made of paper, cloth, or nylon, better capture all the fine particles as well as some percentage of solutes, particularly oils. This might happen because they simply act as a physical barrier that cannot be traversed or it might be that they attract solutes in the brew. Coffees brewed from these filters tend to have lower bodies and flavors that are more poignant or clear, since some confounding molecules have been removed. A trait of some nonmetal filters is that they, too, can be matrices to be extracted. Depending on the filter type, the resulting brew can take on a paper or cloth taste.

> ——— Did you know?
> Coffee drinkers have a lower risk of developing Parkinson's disease, Alzheimer's disease, and type 2 diabetes than non-coffee drinkers.

★ ★ ★

BREWING PARAMETER

CONTAINER TYPE

THE FINAL BREWING PARAMETER IS A BIT LIKE FILTER TYPES; IT DOESN'T INFLUENCE THE EXTRACTION PROCESS BUT IT CAN INFLUENCE THE FINAL TASTE. THIS PARAMETER IS THE CONTAINER TYPE THE BREW IS MADE OR STORED IN. IN A PERFECT WORLD, EVERY CONTAINER THAT COMES IN CONTACT WITH THE COFFEE DURING THE BREWING PROCESS OR AFTERWARDS WOULD BE INERT. IN OTHER WORDS, THE CONTAINER ITSELF WOULDN'T SERVE AS A MATRIX TO BE EXTRACTED. UNFORTUNATELY, THAT ISN'T THE CASE. SOME CONTAINERS CAN IMPART A PLASTIC, METALLIC, OR PAPER TASTE TO THE BREW.

— Did you know? —
Of the 124 species in the genus *Coffea*, only two are grown commercially, *Coffea arabica* and *Coffea canephora*.

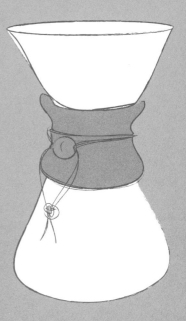

A container made of nonporous heat-resistant glass is likely to have little or no effect on your brew. The hourglass-shaped Chemex Coffeemaker, invented in 1941, is a prominent example.

★ ★ ★

BREWING CHEMISTRY
BRINGING IT ALL TOGETHER

There is no one perfect coffee brewer. The idea is to find one contraption that takes into account all of the sweet spots of each of these brewing parameters and ensures the rules are followed.

COFFEE BREWING IS NOTHING MORE THAN BRINGING THE VARIOUS BREWING PARAMETERS TOGETHER IN HARMONY TO PRODUCE A BEVERAGE THAT IS PLEASING TO DRINK. THE REAL BEAUTY IS THAT NONE OF THEM ARE INDEPENDENT OF EACH OTHER, AS CHANGING ONE MAY NECESSITATE CHANGING ANOTHER.

— Did you know? —
Coffee drinking has a positive effect on liver function while reducing the risks of chronic liver disease and cirrhosis.

For example, if we want a longer contact time, we need to increase the grind size and reduce agitation or increase the brew ratio and increase agitation. If we don't, then too many solutes will be extracted. Alternatively, if we add pressure, then contact time and grind size will need to be adjusted down. By manipulating each parameter just a little, we can have a slightly different resultant brew. This interaction of all the brewing parameters is what allows us to devise so many different ways of brewing coffee.

So, what makes for a great coffee brewer? The easy answer is to say one that takes into account all the sweet spots of the brewing parameters and ensures everything follows the rules. However, just because some contraption can create a fantastic cup of coffee, doesn't necessarily mean it's a great brewer. As any user will tell you, price, ease of use, ease of cleaning, and any number of other factors play a role in the utility of a tool. There are many great coffee brewers that produce fantastic coffee, each one creating a novel representation of the beans that are used. Such diversity, as always, should be celebrated. Perhaps it just means that we ought to have more than one coffee brewer on the kitchen counter!

HOW DO I KNOW

= I GOT IT =

RIGHT?

THE LITTLE COFFEE
KNOW-IT-ALL

IT IS ONE THING TO UNDERSTAND ALL THE UNDERLYING PRINCIPLES TO BREWING COFFEE AND HAVE THE RIGHT BREWER TO EXECUTE THEM, BUT IT IS QUITE ANOTHER TO KNOW IF YOU ACTUALLY BREWED A DECENT CUP! THE SIMPLEST WAY TO FIGURE THIS OUT, OF COURSE, IS TO TASTE THE COFFEE. AFTER ALL, THE TASTER IS THE ARBITER OF QUALITY. ANYONE WITH A LOVE OF SCIENCE, HOWEVER, REALLY WANTS TO PUT SOME NUMBERS TO IT. SO, HOW DO WE QUANTIFY A CORRECT BREW?

The truth is, there is no good way to do this. Taste is the best way to decide and, not only does everyone have a different opinion about what good taste is, but the chemistry of coffee taste is still in its infancy. We don't even know what to quantify!

That said, it isn't like we haven't come up with some proxies to help guide us. After all, if all we've done is a simple chemical extraction, then there ought to be measures of how successful that extraction was. There are two ways to approach this problem. One is to find what percent of solutes were removed from the coffee beans. The other is to measure what percentage of the coffee brew is composed of solutes from coffee beans and not made up of water. Then, all we need to know to make it work is what defines success. Thanks to Dr. Lockhart, we have this information!

Lockhart determined that of the original mass of coffee used for brewing, most people preferred the brews when the extraction yield—the amount of coffee removed from the grounds—was between 18 and 22 percent. So, if we just measure that, will we have a good idea of whether the coffee will taste good? Yes! In practice, though, it is neither very quick

CAFFEINE CONTENT MG/ML – 100% ARABICA

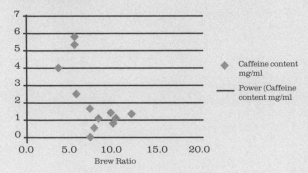

nor practical, so for most people, it is merely a fun idea to think about. The problem is that you can't simply weigh the coffee before you brew, weigh it right after, then divide the former by the latter and subtract it from one. This is because the coffee grounds absorb a substantial amount of water and the added weight throws off the calculation. Instead, you must first slowly dry the coffee grounds in an oven (for about twenty-four hours). Then you can weigh them and add the value into your equation. So, it is doable, but not terribly practical.

Measuring the amount of solutes in the brew is also tricky. To perfectly measure the total dissolved solids (TDS) in the brew, you would have to follow a similar procedure: weigh the total amount of brew, evaporate off the water, and then weigh

> **Did you know?**
>
> **Coffee is not the second most valuable or traded commodity behind petroleum, by any metric.**

the solids that are left behind. After some quick number crunching, you could see if your coffee fell into Lockhart's range of 1.15 percent to 1.35 percent.

Fortunately, there are two quick ways to estimate the TDS in water/coffee. All that is required is the right instrument and the correct calibration. Of course, you probably don't have a conductivity meter or a refractometer at home, but it doesn't mean they wouldn't work if you did have one! Actually, some of these kits aren't too expensive and there are some made specifically for coffee. So, if you're really keen on having such a toy, they are

pretty easy to find.

Pure water conducts a very tiny amount of electricity. However, water that contains ions can conduct electricity quite well (standing in a puddle + lightning = bad). Ions are electrically charged particles that naturally occur. For example, table salt (sodium chloride, NaCl), when dissolved in water, dissociates into its ion components: Na+ and Cl–. Because of their electrical charges, electricity can pass through them readily. The greater the ion concentration is in the water, the greater the electrical conductivity will be. Thus, by measuring the

conductivity of the water, you can get a sense of how many ions are in it. Note, if nonionic species exist in the water, they won't register electrically.

This works for coffee, of course. However, like with any such measurement, you need to have a calibration curve to translate the value for electrical conductivity into TDS. I, for one, don't derive any meaning from a conductivity of 2 mS/cm! Doing this is fairly simple; you just have to plot a graph where the x-axis is conductivity and the y-axis is TDS. You create this graph by measuring the conductivity of several solutions (or brews) that are known to have different TDS (say, by making several cups of weaker and stronger coffee). Hold these values on the x-axis. Then, dry down the brews as described above and once the TDS is known, use the x-axis values to plot against these y-axis points. With three to five points, you'll have a curve (which is actually straight for a good portion of the curve that interests us) that is represented by an equation. That equation is your calibration curve. For any x-value you measure, the equation will produce the y-value TDS!

Now, it is important to measure the TDS by drying down the coffee. As mentioned above, nonionic species won't register. If we don't measure the TDS accurately this way, we'll never have a true correlation between conductivity and TDS because we won't ever be accounting for those nonionic species!

The last little trick with measuring TDS via conductivity is time. If you leave a liquid in the open air (like most of us do with our mugs), it will absorb some carbon dioxide from the air. When this happens, some of the carbon dioxide molecules react with water molecules to become carbonic acid. As acids are ions, this changes the conductivity of the water. So, if you care a lot about the accuracy of your TDS measurement, then do it quickly! The other trick is temperature; conductivity of a liquid changes with temperature. So, for readings to be comparable, you must either always take readings at the same temperature or use an instrument that measures and accounts for temperatures.

Refractometers can also produce values for TDS. They measure the direction in which light moves—its refraction—through a liquid. If you shine a light on a glass of water, it never comes straight out; it always bends a little. If there are dissolved molecules in the water, the amount of bending changes. You can use this bending to calculate the amount of TDS in the liquid. Of course, you need to have a calibration curve to make sense of the reading. Fortunately, refractometers aren't influenced by the absorption of carbon dioxide in the same way TDS meters are. However, their readings are heavily influenced by temperature.

So, there you have it, the knowledge necessary to measure the TDS in your coffee brew. All you need is an instrument and calibration curve (which likely is already built into or calculated by the instrument). Of course, once you know you the TDS of your brew, you need to calibrate that number to your personal preference for the brew. Otherwise, what the heck does TDS mean?

WHY CAN'T I CALL
= IT A =
SIPHON BREWER?

THE LITTLE COFFEE
KNOW-IT-ALL

THERE ARE A VARIETY OF METHODS FOR BREWING COFFEE, EACH MANIPULATING THE BREWING PARAMETERS SLIGHTLY TO PRODUCE A DIFFERENT END RESULT. TO DESCRIBE THEM ALL INDIVIDUALLY WOULD NOT ONLY BE OVERKILL, BUT TEDIOUS AND BORING TO READ. THERE IS ONE METHOD, HOWEVER, THAT WARRANTS A CLOSER LOOK. NOT ONLY DOES IT DRAW UPON SOME OF THE CHEMISTRY/PHYSICS PRINCIPLES DISCUSSED EARLIER, BUT IT IS A FASCINATING AND MESMERIZING BREW METHOD THAT INTRIGUES EVERYONE WHO SEES IT. THIS BREWER, THE VACUUM POT OR SIPHON BREWER, ALSO HAPPENS TO BE A DARLING OF THE SPECIALTY COFFEE INDUSTRY RIGHT NOW.

This beautiful and interesting brew method has been around since before 1827. Often when someone first sees a vacuum pot brewer, they think of laboratory chemistry. The common vertically aligned, two-compartment contraption that begins with water on the bottom and coffee on the top certainly presents an image of scientific mystique. Apply some heat and the water moves to the top chamber, through a tube, and mixes with the coffee. Remove the heat and the now-brewed coffee returns to the lower chamber while the coffee grounds remain on top, thanks to a filter nestled in place at the top of the tube.

All of this sounds very complicated. One might even think the name, siphon pot, alludes to how it works. Unfortunately, no siphoning is occurring using this brew method, making the name rather fallacious. Let's explore just how this brew method works and discover why they should always be called vacuum pots and not siphon pots.

To begin, some physics and chemistry

When enough energy is added to a liquid, the liquid converts into a gas. When enough energy is lost from a gas, it converts into a liquid. When water has reached a temperature of 212°F (100°C), it has enough energy to convert to a gas. For the purposes of this conversation, energy is going to be in the form of heat.

A given amount of liquid takes up less volume than the same amount of it in gaseous form.

The gas phase of an object is less dense than the liquid phase. When the two phases are in the same container, the gas will rise to the top.

A gas that is trapped in a tight space, i.e., one that is under pressure, tries to eliminate that pressure. It will do this by stretching its container (think of plastic wrap on a dish that has been heated on a stove or microwave—it puffs up), moving to a place where it has more space (think of air rushing out of a balloon), or, if there's enough pressure generated, it will break the container (think of a coffee can or brick that wasn't degassed before sealing the container).

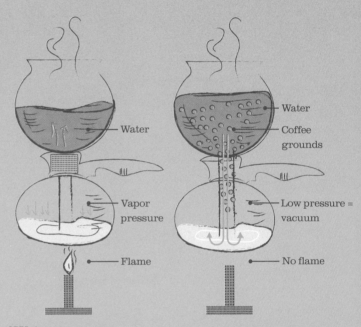

Water

Vapor pressure

Flame

Water

Coffee grounds

Low pressure = vacuum

No flame

STEP 1:
Lifting the water

When heat is added to the water-filled lower compartment (usually via flame, contact with a hot surface, or via a halogen lamp), the energy is transferred to the water molecules. When enough energy is transferred, some of the water molecules convert to a gas (steam). The steam rises to the top of the lower compartment and begins filling up the empty space. Once the upper space is filled, the steam begins exerting pressure on the container wall and the pool of liquid beneath it. When the pressure exceeds that of atmospheric pressure (think of air as filling the space between the ground and outer space; atmospheric pressure is the weight of all that air pushing down on the earth), the steam pushes the liquid water away to make more room for itself. The water only has one place to go—up. It is pushed into the upper compartment through the tube. Note that only the steam is at a temperature of 212°F (100°C); both pools of water are much cooler in the beginning and both will require some time to reach an optimal brew temperature.

As a point of interest, this is similar to the way that electric drip machines move water from their reservoirs to a point above the coffee bed. Electric drip machines heat the water at the bottom of the reservoir, converting some of it to steam. The steam then carries the water to the top of the machine where it escapes through the showerhead.

STEP 2:
Brewing the coffee

Eventually, most of the water is moved to the upper compartment. It is held there by the steam in the lower compartment. Some water remains in the lower

compartment and is a source of new steam. This new steam carries heat to the upper compartment where it will condense and transfer its heat to the pool of water.

Some brewers wait for the upper pool of water to reach proper brewing temperature before adding the coffee while others begin heating the water with the coffee already in the upper compartment. Each of these methods requires its own brewing protocol because of the differences in water temperature, contact time, and agitation. In either method, it is important to remember that the steam will constantly be heating the upper pool of water. Consequently, it is advisable to lower the heat input to limit the amount of heat transferred to the brewing mixture since the water can become too hot and over-extract the coffee.

The influx of new steam to the upper compartment not only transfers heat but it agitates the brew, speeding up the brewing process. Thus, coffee brewed using this method takes less time than most other brewing methods.

STEP 3:
Filtering out the grounds

When the brewer (person, not equipment) decides the brewing is complete, the heat is removed from the lower compartment. As the steam in the lower compartment cools, it condenses back into water. Since the liquid form takes up less volume than the gas, a void is left where the gas was. This void is a partial vacuum that is now at a negative pressure in the lower compartment. The coffee in the upper compartment moves into the lower compartment to equalize the pressure. The filter nestled in the upper compartment permits the water to flow down, but keeps the grounds on the top.

What do we call it?

This method of brewing/brew pot takes its true name from the creation of the partial vacuum: the vacuum pot. I don't know when or where it began, but this brew method gained the additional, erroneous name, siphon pot. It is erroneous because there is no siphoning occurring in this method, no matter what physical shape the pot takes on (there are other shapes where the two compartments are not vertically aligned).

A siphon (noun) is usually a tube or pipe in an upside-down "U" shape. However, the "Ω" is lopsided where one end is much longer than the other. To siphon (verb) is to use the tube to move liquid from a higher location to a lower location, with the liquid moving up the bend and then down to the lower compartment, without the need for a constant input of energy. The short end of the "n" is placed in the higher compartment and the long end in the lower compartment. The process begins with the tube being full of liquid (this is where energy is required), then placed in the starting, higher location. The liquid will flow freely from the lower end of the tube, and, so long as the output end of the tube is below the starting location, the flow of liquid will occur on its own.

Implications for the cup profile

This brew method is a fun presentation of some basic scientific principles. It also tends to be well-regarded as a method of brewing coffee. While the vacuum itself probably doesn't impart any influence on the taste of the beverage, the method does offer two unique aspects that likely do influence the taste.

First, while the coffee is in the upper compartment brewing, the heat from the rising steam allows the temperature to be held constantly at the proper brewing temperature. Other brew methods begin with properly heated water but the water quickly cools as it comes into contact with air and the coffee bed. How this influences the taste has yet to be documented.

Second, there is always a small amount of water that remains in the lower compartment. When the coffee returns to the lower compartment, it mixes with this water and becomes diluted, a process unique to this brewing method. This, too, needs exploration but it seems reasonable to guess that it is analogous to adding a few drops of water to a whisky.

WHAT KIND OF
★ ★ ★
GRINDER
SHOULD I OWN?

Blade grinder

IF PARTICLE SIZE AND SHAPE ARE IMPORTANT TO CREATING A STELLAR CUP OF COFFEE, THEN YOU NEED THE RIGHT TOOL FOR THE JOB. ACHIEVING PERFECT UNIFORMITY OF COFFEE PARTICLES IS IMPOSSIBLE. EVEN THE MOST SOPHISTICATED GRINDERS WILL PRODUCE A RANGE OF DIFFERENT SIZES (THE BETTER THE MACHINES, THE NARROWER THE RANGE). THEREFORE, THE GOAL SHOULD BE TO MINIMIZE THE AMOUNT OF VARIABILITY IN THE PARTICLE SIZES. THERE ARE TWO MAJOR CLASSES OF GRINDERS TO PICK FROM, AND THEY ARE NOT CREATED EQUAL.

The simpler, less effective grinder type that is easily available for grinding coffee is a blade grinder. This grinder type has a metal blade that spins at high velocity in a small chamber. When coffee is in the chamber, the blade chops the beans into smaller and smaller pieces. Since the coffee is trapped in the small chamber, some pieces get chopped more than others. Consequently, there is a significant range of particle sizes in the final product, leading to a less consistent brew extraction.

Another concern about blade grinders is the risk of overheating the bean mass while grinding. Because the coffee is trapped in a small compartment under constant attack by high-speed metal blades, the temperature of the beans is elevated for the duration of the process. This extra heat drives off volatiles (including some we probably want to drink) and possibly, negatively influences the chemical composition of the beans. There's no public research that examines the issue of the grounds heating up but, if it is an issue, then the blade grinder is guilty as charged.

The more complex, effective, and expensive grinder type is a burr grinder. Burr grinders have two metal pieces (burrs) that are maintained a set distance apart from each other. Coffee is added on top of the burrs. As one of the burrs spins, the coffee is ground. When the particle is small enough to fit through the space between the burrs, it falls into a separate chamber below the burrs. Burr

grinders not only achieve a higher uniformity of grind size, but they are easily adjustable, allowing for different grind sizes to be achieved for different purposes. Also, as the beans escape the grinding chamber right away, they aren't subject to as much of an increase in temperature (although, if a large enough mass of beans are being ground, the heat

generated from the burrs will likely be passed on to coffee later down the grind stream).

Both types of grinders have their advantages and disadvantages. As usual, there is no definitive correct answer. In general, consumers concerned about price and having a larger equipment footprint should probably opt for a blade grinder. Whereas a consumer with the available resources who is interested in a higher level of precision to produce a better of cup of coffee should probably acquire a burr grinder.

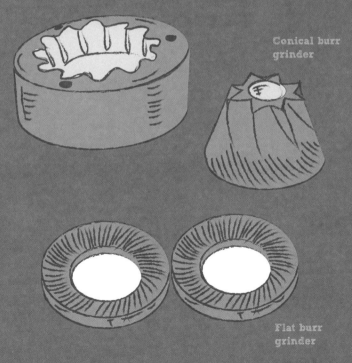

Conical burr grinder

Flat burr grinder

HOW DO I GET THE
★ ★ ★
MOST BUZZ
FROM A CUP?

$$1_{oz} = 6_{oz}$$

Although espressos may have more caffeine per unit of brew, a typical serving of drip brew coffee is so much larger that you can count on its total caffeine content being greater.

LET'S BE HONEST, NO COFFEE DRINKER IS COMPLETELY INNOCENT. AT ONE TIME OR ANOTHER, WE'VE EACH HAD A CUP OF COFFEE NOT FOR THE SHEER PLEASURE OF IT BUT FOR THE SHEER NEED OF IT. SOMETIMES, IT IS ALL ABOUT CAFFEINE. ONCE WE ACCEPT THAT IT ISN'T ALWAYS ABOUT THE FLAVOR, WE BEGIN TO WONDER, THEN, WHAT KIND OF INFLUENCE BREWING HAS ON JUST HOW MUCH CAFFEINE ENDS UP IN THE CUP.

After all, if it is the caffeine we want, we might as well figure out how to get the most into each cup! With brewing, there are two main things to consider: brew method and filter type. Before we discuss those, let's discuss solubility a bit. For every molecule, we can measure its solubility. Solubility is the amount of the molecule that can dissolve in a set amount of liquid at a given temperature. We're interested, of course, in caffeine's solubility in water. Caffeine is a little soluble in water at room temperature 73°F (23°C), about 16 mg caffeine/1 ml water. As the temperature of the water increases to 176°F (80°C) and 212°F (100°C) (boiling), the solubility jumps up to approximately 200 mg/ml and 666 mg/ml, respectively! What a great demonstration about how important temperature is to discussions of solubility!

When trying to figure out how much caffeine can potentially end up in a cup of coffee, it helps to know how much is in the roasted coffee to start with. The values for this vary quite a bit. In one study of an arabica collection in Ethiopia, the caffeine content ranged from .42 to 2.9 percent! Let's use 1.15 percent for our calculation, using 20 g of coffee and 360 ml water. That 20 g of coffee contains 230 mg of caffeine. Since 360 ml of water at room temperature can dissolve 5760 mg of caffeine, it is possible to get all of that caffeine into the resulting approximately 11 oz cup of coffee. For myriad reasons, all the caffeine doesn't come out during brewing, though most of it does. The two main reasons not all the caffeine is removed are that some of the caffeine will be preferentially attracted to the bean matrix over the solvent and that some water always remains in the bean mass (and will retain the same dissolved solids that the water in the cup also has).

Knowing we can extract most of the caffeine from the beans, is there a difference between brew methods in how effective they are? The answer is yes, although, unfortunately, we can only hypothesize as to why some of the differences exist; no researchers have published the "why" of caffeine differences, only the "what".

The espresso brew method results in a brew that has a higher concentration of caffeine than any other brew method. One study shows a concentration of nearly twice as much compared to American drip, Neapolitan flip, and the Moka pot. Unpublished research by this author showed an almost seven times increase in concentration using espresso brewing! In general, methods that use hot water and no additional pressure don't differ in their caffeine concentrations from each other. Coffee made using an Aeropress has a concentration somewhere between espresso and the other methods.

This leads one to think that pressure may be the important difference—it removes more caffeine and/or forces more water out of the beans. However, both the Aeropress and espresso use much lower water-to-coffee ratios than nonpressurized brew methods; they may have more caffeine because more coffee was used! However, other brewing parameters are at play here, too. Finer grinding, when producing small batches of coffee (single cup versus full pot), increases the concentration.

Filters also influence the concentration by intercepting the caffeine as it passes through them. One Brazilian study compared the effect using five different types of filters had on the caffeine concentration of the final brew. The results indicated highest concentrations using a nylon filter, followed by white paper, then brown, unbleached paper and cotton, with flannel yielding the lowest concentrations. In some contradiction, unpublished research by this author showed no difference in concentration using a paper filter or a gold metal filter.

For the practical coffee drinker, an important thing to keep in mind is not just the difference in caffeine concentrations but the total caffeine intake per unit. The classic case is espresso verses drip. In the United States, most serving sizes of espresso are 1 to 2 ounces (29.5 to 59 ml) whereas a cup of drip can be 12 to 16 ounces (355 to 473 ml). So, while espresso may have more caffeine per unit of brew, a normal serving of drip is so much larger that its final content of caffeine is typically much greater than that small serving of espresso. The same is true for the filters. While there was a mathematical difference in the concentrations, sometimes the difference was small enough that a person's body might not recognize the difference as being physiologically important.

PART FOUR
THE CUP

**THE LITTLE COFFEE
KNOW-IT-ALL**

WHAT'S THE BEST
★ ★ ★
COFFEE IN
THE WORLD?

THE LITTLE COFFEE
KNOW-IT-ALL

WOULDN'T IT BE SPECTACULAR IF THERE WERE AN ANSWER TO THIS QUESTION? WHAT IF WE COULD ALL POINT TO ONE COFFEE AND SAY, "THIS IS THE WORLD'S BEST COFFEE AND EVERYONE WILL LOVE IT." HOW LOVELY IT WOULD BE FOR FARMERS, BROKERS, AND ROASTERS, WHO WOULD ALL HAVE A MODEL OF PERFECTION TO WHICH THEY COULD ASPIRE. HOW EASY IT WOULD BE FOR EVERY BARISTA TO RECOMMEND A COFFEE FOR THAT SPECIAL GIFT. ALAS, THERE WILL NEVER BE A UNIVERSAL ANSWER TO THAT QUESTION.

The reason why is simple. There is no single flavor profile that everybody is going to think is the best coffee they've ever drunk. What would that coffee taste like? The millions (billions?) of coffee drinkers on the planet surely will all have something a bit different to say about it. How should it be processed? At what roast level should it be? Should it have lots of complexity and nuance or just really taste like coffee?

There is no goldilocks coffee. There is no way to define quality in a way that suits every person, every time. Rather, there are many "best" coffees in the world. Preference is subjective and this means diversity is something to celebrate. Thus, the only sufficient answer to this question is "whatever coffee you like the most."

The only way to talk about quality in an absolute sense is if it is first defined. This means laying out all the organoleptic characteristics and assigning them the desired intensity. One way to do this is to establish a scale of 1 to 10 where the range represents "not present" to "so present no other coffee can have more of this". Then, each characteristic and descriptor is assigned a score: acidity = 3, body = 8, floral = 6…. Once a definition is established, there can be a standard by which to measure and thus a best coffee or a winner in a competition. Until then, "best" is always a moving target.

After a definition is created, we can do cool things like taste any coffee in the world and say whether it is good or not good relative to that standard. All we have to do is compare its intensity values to the standard (this is trickier than it sounds, but not impossible). To make

described by a normal curve. This is all statistical lingo that represents, effectively, a way of mathematically representing our graph. The value to us is that we can assign numerical values to the area under the curve. In other words, if the total area under the curve equals 1, then each category takes up some percentage of that total area. Consequently, if we wanted to know the probability of randomly selecting a bad coffee from our population, it would be 2.1 percent.

One of the best uses of the bell curve of quality is to give us perspective on how much spectacular coffee exists in the world based on our assumptions (seven categories and a normal distribution). The value is 0.1 percent! Of course, we can take this bell curve and apply it to a country, a region, or a city in the United States... Sure, the shape of the curve might change and we can alter how many standard deviations we want to consider, but the idea stays the same.

Personally, I'm not interested in the best coffee in the world. Diversity is a good thing and having variety is my subjective preference. Besides, if the whole planet of coffee farmers is our population from which to choose, in even just 0.1 percent of the samples are a lot of spectacular coffees for me to enjoy!

communication simpler, we can make arbitrary categories like horrible, bad, poor, acceptable, good, great, and spectacular that all describe how far away a particular coffee is from the standard.

We can get really geeky and graph the probability of randomly picking a coffee of a particular quality from a set of coffees. To do this, we first need a set, or a population, of samples from which to make our selections. Let's say our population is composed of all the coffee farms in a country and a randomly picked sample is a single farm.

Our graph will have two axes. The x-axis (horizontal) will be "quality" with movement towards the right getting us closer to the standard we've defined and the far left being a level of quality as far away from that standard as possible. The y-axis (vertical) will be "number of farms." If we plot our population on the graph, it will look like a bell curve where the tail end on the left represents horrible, the tail end on the right represents spectacular, and the other categories fall into place in the middle.

The areas under the curve that our categories represent are not chosen arbitrarily. Rather, they are standard deviations from the mean (the very center of the curve, a.k.a, the average). For this to work, we have to assume that our population is

WHY DOES THIS COFFEE ★ ★ TASTE ★ ★ DIFFERENT THAN IT DID LAST TIME?

THE LITTLE COFFEE
KNOW-IT-ALL

WHY DOES THIS COFFEE TASTE DIFFERENT THAN IT DID LAST TIME?

WE HAVE AN EXPECTATION THAT A SINGLE BAG OF COFFEE SHOULD PRODUCE CUPS OF COFFEE THAT ALL TASTE THE SAME. YET, MORE OFTEN THAN NOT, WE BELIEVE THAT THE CUP OR POT WE BREWED YESTERDAY TASTED DIFFERENT THAN IT DID TODAY. THE FREAKY THING IS THAT IT PROBABLY DID TASTE DIFFERENTLY YESTERDAY. IS IT POSSIBLE THAT THE COFFEE DID CHANGE SINCE YESTERDAY OR ARE WE JUST CRAZY? DEPENDING ON THE DAY, MAYBE BOTH.

Let's start with the coffee and figure out how the coffee itself could be different day to day. We already know that coffee stales just a little bit everyday and that if it is already ground, the process happens at a much faster rate. But is it really that fast a process? Probably not, at least, not so fast that we can tell after just one day.

What we always assume, though, is that the bag or can of coffee is perfectly homogenous, that is, every bean inside is nearly identical. The truth is, that rarely happens. Sometimes, bad beans make it into the lot. These beans are usually bad from the start—they were picked that way or they processed poorly and were mixed in with good coffee. While there are many ways of sorting out bad beans (hand picking, screening by size, separating by density, and color sorting) none of them are perfect. Bad beans will always sneak through the system.

Sometimes, you can see these beans in a bag of whole bean coffee. They often are discolored (usually lighter) but really junk ones can be all black. Some are broken or have evident insect damage. These beans are more difficult to see and taste in darker roasted coffees, but some can still leave their mark on the cup. Every so often, though, beans that make it past all the sorting and look just fine in the roasted bag still end up tasting a bit off from the rest.

Generally, there aren't very many of these beans. So, the odds of one getting into any given pot are low. Even if it did make it into a pot, if it were just one bean, it would probably be so diluted as to be unrecognizable. As an extension, a bag of ground beans are likely to be much more homogenous as they'll be able to mix much better. If you are brewing just one cup at a time, though (an increasingly common practice), a single bean can make an incredibly big difference. So, it might just be the case that one bad bean spoils the whole cup, making today's cup different than yesterday's.

Hopefully, though, that doesn't happen too often, which suggests that differences in how our coffee tastes day to day are due to something in our heads. We are thinking, feeling creatures who use our brains to process *everything*. Whether it is a translation of the electrical signal received after

---

Did you know?

A pound (455 g) of medium roasted coffee will be composed of 2,800–4,725 coffee beans (depending on their density).

Stage	For 1 lb (455 g) roasted coffee...	% of weight
Cherry	5.9 lb (2.7 kg)	100
Parchment	1.5 lb (680 g)	25
Green	1.2 lb (544 g)	20
Roasted	1 lb (455 g)	17

─── **Did you know?** ───

To produce 1 pound (455 g) of roasted coffee, at least
6.5 pounds (3 kg) of coffee cherry must be picked.

a sugar molecule interacts with a taste bud or the frustration from the cat leaving a carcass in the hallway, or our brain interpreting the gestalt of the experience of an incredible cup of coffee, it is all dependent upon our psychology and how our brains work. So, we're not actually crazy; we're just human. And this means all kinds of explanations exist to explain this inconsistent coffee phenomenon!

One explanation to explore is that we rely too much on our sense of perfection while measuring things. Specifically, we aren't all so good at measuring weight, volume, and temperature. Moreover, many household measuring tools (measuring cups and spoons, specifically) aren't as precise as we may need them to be and let's not even start about the measured lines printed into coffee pots. It is quite likely that in our overconfidence, we measure the water, the coffee, or the water temperature differently day to day. This would certainly produce cups that taste differently enough to recognize. Fortunately, the solution is pretty simple: weigh everything. We talked about brew ratios in a previous section. If you weigh the coffee and the water, your level of consistency will skyrocket (FYI, 1 milliliter of water

weighs 1 gram. Thus, you can exchange volume for weight if you're measuring using the metric system). If you heat your own water, use a thermometer. There's no reason to guess and have variable tasting coffee when cheap, simple tools will solve the problem.

Let's be honest, mismeasuring water isn't something we really want to blame on us being human. It is really more about being lazy and ill-equipped than anything else. The truth is, we are subject to the whims of our psychology in very real ways.

It might just be that we have bad memories. I don't mean that we just don't quite remember what we tasted last time but that we actually have really terrible memories. Even though we feel confident that we remember specific details about things, we often get them wrong. More frighteningly, it is easy to create memories in people of things they have never experienced. To top it off, every time we remember things that are actual memories, we change them ever so slightly. It may not be that the coffee is different at all, rather, you're just remembering it differently!

Aside from having lousy memories, our ability to taste is heavily influenced by so many external factors. We should all be wary of how we interpret our eating experiences because of how susceptible we are to the world around us. For example, the color of ambient light influences how much we like a wine and how much we'd be willing to pay for it (blue and red lights produced higher ratings than white and green lights). We're also influenced by the color of the dish or cup, the colors of food on the dish, and the colors around us.

Ambient sounds are incredibly influential on perceptions of foods, including the sound of the food itself (e.g., the crunch of a potato chip or the sizzle of carbonated water), the sound of the packaging, the sound of machines, the sound of music, and the sound of the sea. To name a couple specific to us, coffee aroma is rated higher when the drinker can hear someone else who is drinking coffee rather than someone eating a potato chip. The quality of the sound of the coffee machine influences how much we enjoy the coffee as well (bad sounding machines cause us to like the coffee less).

Our sense of touch can make us think differently about how things taste. The texture of packaging changes our mind about food as does the weight of the dish. Even the material a spoon is coated with will make us rate the food somewhat differently. Research combining a variety of environmental cues on the perception of whiskey demonstrates that our mind doesn't focus on just one influence at a time, but is bombarded by them all!

Not only do environmental cues trick us into thinking differently about how we taste, but so does our emotional state. Being in love, in a positive or negative mood, or depressed will make you think differently about what's happening in your mouth. It is likely that other emotions can influence our organoleptic responses.

It is evident that we are lousy instruments. Although we may not be conscious of it, many little, seemingly insignificant things actually have a significant impact on how we experience foods and beverages. Considering this, it is no surprise at all that coffee can taste differently from one day to the next. It may not be the coffee that's different; it may be you!

> **Did you know?**
> The first commercial espresso machine was produced in 1905 by Desiderio Pavoni.

HOW CAN I
= OUTSMART =
MY OWN HEAD?

IT IS PRETTY CLEAR THAT OUR MINDS INTERNALIZE EXTERNAL STIMULI TO SUCH AN EXTENT THAT THEY INFLUENCE HOW WE PERCEIVE TASTE. OUR EMOTIONS, TOO, TWEAK OUR INTERPRETATIONS OF TASTE. ARE THERE OTHER MENTAL PITFALLS THAT WE HAVE THAT WE SHOULD AVOID IF WE'RE TRYING TO GET THE CLEAREST, MOST OBJECTIVE TASTE RESPONSE POSSIBLE? THE ANSWER, OF COURSE, IS YES! SENSORY SCIENTISTS UNDERSTAND THESE PITFALLS WELL AND HAVE DEVISED METHODS TO AMELIORATE OR ELIMINATE THEM.

These psychological errors are most pertinent for professional coffee cuppers and judges in competitions. Being aware of these pitfalls can help them design their evaluations to be more accurate and less susceptible to human errors. However, everyday drinkers, who probably don't end up in formal evaluation settings, may find this list superfluous.

Nonetheless, anyone keen to take their sensory experience to the next level will find themselves behaving differently once they know what to avoid!

These psychological errors go by different names in different sources. So, if you read about them elsewhere, be prepared for the confusion. Here they are in no particular order:

Order of presentation errors

First sample effect—When several samples are presented simultaneously, tasters may rate the first sample higher or lower than they would if it were in a different position.

Contrast effect—If adjacent samples are highly contrasted (e.g., one high quality then one

The order in which the samples are presented to you and your prior knowledge of the brews are just two factors that may have dramatic effects on your evaluation of taste. Being aware of these pitfalls will make your evaluations less susceptible to human error.

low quality), the second sample may get scored abnormally lower (and vice versa if the low quality sample is presented first).

Group effect—Opposite to the contrast effect, if one type of sample is placed amongst a group of different samples, the single sample is more likely to be rated like the rest of the group.

Central tendency effect— Samples placed in the center of a group of samples tend to be preferred more than the outer samples.

Pattern effect—Assessors may look for patterns amongst the samples, and, if discovered, may be biased.

For an individual, little can be done to avoid these errors, though training will help. When

working with a larger group, the errors can be balanced across the whole group. Samples must be presented in a different, random order to each person. If every person receives a different first sample or a different middle sample, then the biases for those spots will be averaged across all the samples.

expectation can be prevented by drinking your coffee (or other beverage) without knowing anything about it. This means that coffee professionals should not look at the beans, either in the green or roasted state, prior to or during evaluation of a brew.

Stimulus error

This is similar to the error of expectation. If a taster has prior knowledge of a product that is unrelated to the actual product, they will likely score a product in error. If you are going to drink a coffee from a well-regarded roaster, you'll likely rate the coffee higher. A famous study showed that drinkers will rate a wine higher and describe it more positively if it comes from a Grand Cru bottle rather than a table wine bottle. To prevent this, tasters should be occluded from all information about a product.

Error of habituation

We are creatures of habit. If you are presented samples that are systematically changed, albeit slowly, then you tend to proffer the same rating. Thus, if a coffee that has been roasted ever so darker or lighter is presented each day, a taster may not discern it and will consequently score each successive coffee like the ones before it.

> **Did you know?**
> The first U.S. patent for decaffeinating coffee was applied for in 1906 and issued in 1908.

Error of central tendency

This is just like the central tendency effect, only it applies not to a sample within a group of samples but to the rating of a characteristic of a sample. If rating the intensity of a characteristic, such as sweetness, a person is more likely to score the sample in the middle of the scale instead of near the ends. We have a mental fear of the extremes, it seems. Extensive training can help prevent this error by helping us not only become comfortable with the extreme ends of scales, but with recognizing the whole range of the scale itself.

Error of expectation

You find what you're looking for. If you know you are drinking a dark roasted coffee, you'll find flavors associated with dark roasts. Similarly, if a nearby person makes a sound or gesture after tasting the coffee, you'll expect to find something. A good example of this was demonstrated by coloring a white wine with an odorless red dye before inviting tasters to smell the wine and identify what general type of wine they were drinking. A large percentage of the group was tricked and labeled the wine as red wine, despite their sensory experience of the aroma. Errors of

Logical error

These occur when tasters associate two or more characteristics together, which may or may not be associated. For example, lighter roasted coffees are associated with higher acidity. Thus, independent of the actual acidity of a coffee, tasters are likely to rate it higher because of the roast level. This is pretty difficult to avoid in some cases. Eliminating any not-gustatory sensory experiences can help. In the case of this example, nullifying the visual cue of the roast level by serving the samples in red light may help. Ultimately, tasters must be trained away from this error.

Halo effect

Sometimes the rating of one characteristic can influence the rating of another characteristic, even when they are completely unrelated. The most serious transgression is when a taster is asked to rate the intensity of a characteristic and their liking for the product. Their subjective response will almost always influence the other ratings, just as you'd expect it to: the more a sample is liked, the higher the scores will be. This happens whether the taster's preference is asked as the first or last question. This is why sensory tests should either be preference-based or descriptive-based, but never both.

Dumping effect

When asked to rate specific characteristics, tasters are limited by the choices given to them. If some other flavor is present but there's no place to rate it, it may distract them to the point of changing the intensity of one of the options that is presented to them. Thus, they dump the experience incorrectly on an available trait. This is best avoided by having proper prior knowledge of a product and including all the relative characteristics on the score sheet. Unfortunately, for sensorially complex foods like coffee, there may simply be too many characteristics in the experience that putting them all on a score sheet is impractical. In fact, asking tasters to rate too many characteristics seems to produce the opposite effect, causing tasters to become inhibited and underrate characteristics.

Did you know?

In 2012, Brazil produced more green coffee than the next five largest producers combined.

WHY DOES THE BAG
★ SAY ★
WOOD AND SPICE
BUT I TASTE EARTHY?

THE LITTLE COFFEE
KNOW-IT-ALL

IT HAPPENS ALL THE TIME. YOU PICK UP A BOTTLE OF WINE BECAUSE THE TAG DESCRIBES THE TASTE AS PLUM AND ANISE OR YOU BREAK OPEN A BAG OF COFFEE BECAUSE IT SAYS IT SHOULD TASTE LIKE CLOVE, MELON, AND PEPPER. THEN, WHEN YOU DRINK IT, YOU DON'T TASTE ANY OF THOSE THINGS! IN FACT, SOMETIMES THE EXPERIENCE IS COMPLETELY DIFFERENT. WHAT'S GOING ON? WE CAN'T HELP BUT WONDER WHAT THE TASTERS AND WRITERS WERE THINKING. WERE THEY JUST INVENTING INTERESTING, ROMANTIC TERMS TO STICK ON THE LABEL TO LURE US INTO A PURCHASE, OR IS THERE PERHAPS SOMETHING MORE AT PLAY?

There are a bunch of reasons why what the consumer tastes could be different from what the expert, purveyor, or advertiser tastes. The business of translating a sensory experience from one person to another is tricky and difficult and it is certainly never perfect. The worst part about the taste incongruity is that while the descriptions on the bag of coffee and the tastes a consumer identifies may be completely different, they can both be entirely correct! Here are a few reasons why.

Experts are, well, experts. When a person spends a lifetime studying and practicing something, they get good at it. People who taste for a living learn to pay attention to subtle flavors and they learn to verbalize an enormous range of experiences. Sometimes, they detect flavors that the average person cannot detect or verbalize. Unfortunately, they can't always tell what is easy to detect and what isn't. So, they can end up listing descriptors that other people can miss.

Not all tasters are good at their job. We want to believe that the person getting paid to taste and write descriptions is very good. This isn't always the case. They may be putting the wrong word to an experience or have a limited vocabulary, which hinders the precision of their word choice.

Humans are lousy instruments. People are heavily influenced by culture, history, experience, emotion, psychology, physiology, and their immediate environment. It makes humans fascinating creatures but terrible at identifying and describing organoleptic experiences: A taster may detect a flavor one day but not another; they may not have tasted the spice or fruit that could be used to describe the coffee; they may value a flavor differently than someone else and thus report it differently; they may just be physically unable to taste that flavor; they may be sick; they may have just had a spicy meal…. On top of all this, it isn't just the taster who suffers from being human, but the consumer, too!

Analytical assessment is different than drinking coffee normally. Professional coffee tasters create environments that help them be more accurate in their evaluation. If their precision is too high, the person drinking at home, using different brewing parameters under different conditions may not have the same advantage of precision as the professional.

Coffee is dynamic. Most professional tasters evaluate the coffee within a day or two of roasting. Most consumers get it days, if not weeks, after that. In all that time, coffee is changing. It may simply be that the flavors listed on a package are no longer there!

Brewing parameters influence the taste of brewed coffee. It is very likely the brewing parameters used by the taster were different than what the consumer uses. In fact, what are the odds that they are identical for the taster and consumer? We spent a whole section discussing how water quality, water temperature, and other brewing parameters influence the final taste of a coffee. It is likely that the taste of the coffee is, in fact, different!

Verbalizing organoleptic experiences is challenging. Sometimes, tasters use words that represent feelings, colors, places, ideas, and experiences. These aren't always helpful to the consumer, even other professionals. Still, a person is limited by their abilities and their attempts to be clear and precise may become so creative as to not always translate well to other drinkers.

With all these complications, can we ever trust the descriptors? Certainly! The descriptors aren't incorrect, they are just one person's (or a few people's) interpretations of the coffee. It is not impossible for both the writer and the drinker to agree on the tastes! In cases where the consumer may not detect any of the flavors described, it can at least give them an idea of the coffee's potential. In addition, those descriptors can also help guide the consumer in their quest to become better tasters. Knowing those flavors are there will often help consumers taste them. Sure, it can just be bias, but sometimes it is just giving the person the right word to match the experience.

HOW COME MY TEXTBOOK = GOT THE = TONGUE MAP WRONG?

THE LITTLE COFFEE
KNOW-IT-ALL

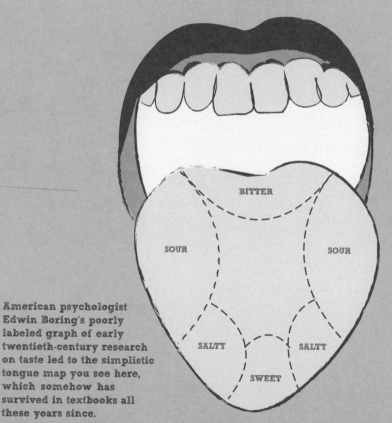

BITTER

SOUR

SOUR

SALTY

SALTY

SWEET

American psychologist Edwin Boring's poorly labeled graph of early twentieth-century research on taste led to the simplistic tongue map you see here, which somehow has survived in textbooks all these years since.

IT HARDLY SEEMS RIGHT TO TAKE A SIMPLE, BEAUTIFUL FACT THAT WE LEARNED AS CHILDREN AND TEAR IT AWAY FOR THE SAKE OF TRUTH. BUT, THAT'S WHAT IS GOING TO HAPPEN HERE. MOREOVER, IT DOESN'T PERTAIN TO COFFEE SPECIFICALLY, BUT TO TASTE IN GENERAL.

Remember the map of the tongue that showed how different regions of the tongue perceive specific tastes? The one with sour in the back and on the sides and sweet on the tip? Well, it is wrong, and it always has been wrong. Not only is the mapping of tastes wrong, but it never even included all the tastes our tongues can perceive!

The story begins in 1901 when the German scientist D.P. Hänig published a paper on the sensitivity of parts of the tongue to the four basic tastes (sweet, sour, bitter, and salt). He demonstrated that the tastes were perceived everywhere but that their intensities varied by region. In 1942, a famous psychologist, Edwin Boring, translated that paper, did some calculations, made a graph, and published it in his classic psychology text. Unfortunately, he didn't label his graph well, so readers, quite understandably, misinterpreted what he was saying and they proceeded to make the false tongue map that we all know and no longer love.

In 1974, Virginia Collings tried to replicate Hänig's work. While some of her data disagreed with his, she was able to support his original thesis—that the tongue's sensitivity to different tastes varied across regions. I suspect she then realized the tongue map was wrong and traced it back to Boring. Unfortunately, I cannot begin to surmise how the simplistic tongue map has managed to survive all the years since then!

It is now well established, even at the cellular level, that not only are the tastes perceived all around the tongue, but that some types of taste buds will respond to more than one taste. What we also know is that, conclusively, there is a fifth taste, umami. Umami is not a well-recognized flavor in Western food culture but it is very familiar in Asia, where it was discovered.

Umami was discovered in 1909 by a Japanese researcher, K. Ikeda. He worked with a traditional soup base, called dashi, which is made from kelp (seaweed). The taste is usually described as meaty, brothy, or savory and is evinced by the amino acid glutamic acid or its dissociated versions, glutamates. Ikeda discovered the technique to produce a salt for commercial purposes. We know it as monosodium glutamate. Between the lack of experience with this taste and the fact that the original research paper was written in Japanese, it took a long time before Western sensory scientists accepted umami as a taste.

Researchers are currently debating the existence of a sixth taste, fatty. So, we may need to revisit the topic of the tongue's tasting abilities. Of course, most of what we think of as flavor is actually derived from smell, which explains the diversity of flavors we perceive. But, that's a topic for another book.

IS THAT CHEESE
★ ★ ★
IN MY COFFEE?

Because whether or not milk curdles in your coffee is so dependent on slight variations of both the temperature and acidity of the coffee, there's little you can do to prevent it.

IT DOESN'T HAPPEN OFTEN BUT EVERY ONCE IN AWHILE, SOMEONE POURS MILK OR ALTERNATIVE MILK (LIKE SOYMILK) INTO THEIR COFFEE AND FLUFFY, WHITE CHUNKS APPEAR AND FLOAT TO THE SURFACE. THOSE CHUNKS, PRECURSORS TO CHEESE, CERTAINLY DESTROY ANY DESIRE TO DRINK THE COFFEE. AT LEAST, THEY WOULDN'T APPEAL TO ME! WHEN THOSE CHUNKS APPEAR, WE COMMONLY SAY THE MILK CURDLED WHEREAS SCIENTISTS USE THE TERM COAGULATED.

Those chunks are proteins that were always present in the milk but were shaped and dispersed in such a way that they were tiny, suspended groups, rather than large, aggregated chunks. It isn't until we disrupt their natural environment that they come to the surface. The proteins are perfectly normal

and, in fact, are part of what makes milk (and alt milks) a good nutritional source. Other food items contain proteins that go from states of being dissolved to being coagulated. For example, think egg whites that begin as clear in raw eggs but turn white upon heating or severe beating.

Proteins are just long chains of amino acids that fold up in very complex, specific ways. If you take a piece of string and crumpled it in your hand, you'll get an idea of how a protein might look. In a protein, that shape is held together by a variety of bonds at the atomic level, none of which are incredibly strong and thus are prone to disruption. If the bonds are disrupted, then, in most cases, the protein will denature (lose its shape) and come out of solution. In other words, it becomes a solid and is no longer part of the liquid. There are a few ways to disrupt those bonds; in the case of milk and coffee, the most important disruption is acidity.

Acidity in a liquid is a measure of the concentration of hydrogen ions present in the liquid. The pH scale helps us talk about the concentration in easy numbers as well as give us an indication of whether hydrogen ions dominate a solution (as in an acid solution) or if bases dominate a solution (an alkaline solution). In solutions with a pH below 7 (as measured on the pH scale of 0 to 14), hydrogen ions dominate. A solution with a pH above 7 has a greater concentration of hydroxide ions (the counterpart ion species of a base). Solutions with a pH of 7 (pure water, by definition) have an equal balance of hydrogen and hydroxide ions.

When proteins are in a solution, they can maintain their shape around a certain pH. In other words, the bonds holding its shape together are affected by the relative concentration of hydrogen ions. Casein, the primary protein in cow's milk, will remain in solution at pH above 4.6. As the pH approaches that number, coagulation begins. The pH of black coffee varies somewhat but it tends to be around 5. Thus, milk doesn't usually coagulate in coffee. The magic pH for soy proteins is a bit higher, around 4.9. Thus, unadulterated soymilk tends to coagulate in coffee.

There are a few reasons why milk will coagulate in coffee. One, the pH of the coffee may actually be near 4.6. Two, the milk being added might already be near that pH, normally due to lack of freshness where bacteria helped bring it down. Fresh milk has a pH around 6.7. However, as it ages, different bacteria consume molecules in the milk and produce acids as byproducts that we recognize as a sour taste. Most notable of these critters are lactic acid bacteria, which ferment lactose (the primary carbohydrate in milk) into lactic acid. However, they're mostly active at room temperature. Other bacteria grow just fine in refrigerated conditions, though, including pseudomonads, enterobacteria, and *Paenibacillus*. As the acid concentration increases, the pH of the milk decreases. The lower the pH, the more likely mixing it with coffee will precipitate the proteins as the overall hydrogen ion concentration increases. As an aside, this is why spoiled milk curdles; the pH drops low enough to coagulate the protein!

To make matters more interesting, milk curdling is temperature dependent; milk can be at or near a pH of 4.6 and not coagulate, as long as it is cold. The moment the temperature rises, when the milk touches the hot coffee, the proteins coagulate. Nature designed caseins to coagulate at the temperature of babies' stomachs.

There's little one can do to prevent milk from curdling if the milk or coffee is particularly acidic. If the milk is getting old, acquiring fresher milk may solve the problem. Alternative milks, however, can't be fixed by the consumer. Manufacturers of alt milks, fortunately, are aware of this problem and they solve it by adding buffers to their product. Buffers are molecules that can maintain the pH of a solution when an acid or base is added. Thus, instead of the acid in the coffee denaturing the proteins, the acid is captured by the buffer up to a point (eventually, the buffer is consumed and the pH will begin dropping). Of course, if these alt milks are of low microbial quality, they too will eventually coagulate.

At the end of the day, there's only one guaranteed method to prevent milks from coagulating in the coffee. Don't use them! Drink it black, instead.

CAN I DRINK COFFEE
= WHEN I'M =
IN OUTER SPACE?

THE LITTLE COFFEE
KNOW-IT-ALL

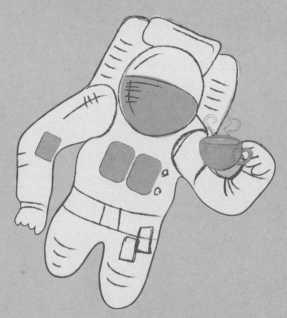

Drinking coffee is pretty simple, as long as you have gravity on your side. In space, astronauts have begun replacing straws with an airplane wing shaped cup, which better replicates the coffee sipping experience.

IF YOU'VE MADE IT THIS FAR IN THE BOOK, THEN YOU PROBABLY HAVE AN APPRECIABLE LOVE OF SCIENCE. IF YOU LOVE SCIENCE THAT MUCH, THEN YOU ALMOST CERTAINLY WANT TO TAKE A TRIP TO SPACE. HOW COOL WOULD THAT BE!? WELL, YOU'LL BE GLAD TO KNOW THAT YOU DON'T HAVE TO KICK YOUR HABIT WHEN YOU GO; THE CHALLENGES OF COFFEE IN SPACE ARE SOLVED, OR AT LEAST, WILL PROBABLY BE SOLVED BY THE TIME YOU GET THERE.

There have been two major challenges with coffee in space: brewing and drinking. Sure, you can just take up instant coffee and drink through a straw, but if you're going to commit to the expense of space travel, a little luxury from back home would be preferred.

We tend to think brewing coffee is pretty simple: pour

hot water over ground coffee and let it trickle down into the pot, fully immerse the coffee in hot water, or push pressurized water through the bed of coffee. Well, it is pretty simple, if you have a little thing called gravity on your side. Without gravity, liquids don't pour because there's no gravity bringing them down. Also, liquids behave oddly in space because of the absence of gravity. So, getting the water and coffee to mix properly is no small feat. There's also the problem of steam bubbles, which are generated by heating the water. On Earth, they distribute evenly in a body of water before rising to the top. In space, they congregate and create a massive, very hot air bubble—a tricky thing to deal with in a machine and on a tiny space station.

Two solutions have been invented. One, designed by Costa Rican engineering students in 2008, garnered some international media attention. However, neither the machine nor the students seemed to convince the right people to try out their machine.

In 2014, two Italian companies and the Italian Space Agency teamed up to design and build an espresso machine that would function in space and produce high-quality espresso. Unfortunately, again because of the gravity issue, the espresso won't have a layer of crema riding on the top, rather it will likely be intermixed with the brew. The machine, dubbed ISSpresso, was delivered to the International Space Station on April 17, 2015.

The lack of gravity in space creates a problem with drinking as well. Not only can you not pour coffee into a cup, but you can't pour it into your mouth. For many years, astronauts have been relegated to using straws for all their drinking, no matter what the temperature of the liquid. Apparently, after you spend some quality time in space, you wish straws weren't the only way to drink, especially with hot liquids.

The recently invented solution is a cup shaped like an airplane's wing. It has a rounded side opposite a side that forms a crease. In a zero-gravity

environment, liquid won't flow of its own volition, but it will move by capillary action along a crease.

Capillary action results from weak electrical interactions between molecules that cause one molecule to drag a molecule along with it if it isn't being pulled too hard and the molecules are in a tight space. It is kind of like a conga line, where a person is holding onto the shoulders of someone in front of them and they have a person behind them holding their shoulders. If the tug from the front is just right, everybody gets pulled along and the line moves. But if the tug is too hard, the line breaks and there's no more movement. This is how water is thought to move up through plants: all the water in a plant is connected and it is slowly dragged upwards. As water in a leaf evaporates, the water behind it replaces it and drags all the other water up with it. It is a bit more complicated than this, of course, but it is the general idea. In the space cup, the pull of the liquid originates with the drinker, sucking the liquid from the crease. As they suck, the liquid is dragged along the crease, giving an astronaut a more familiar drinking experience.

WHY DOES COFFEE
★ ★ SEND ME ★ ★
STRAIGHT TO
THE BATHROOM?

THE LITTLE COFFEE
KNOW IT-ALL

WHEN MOST OF US HEAR THIS QUESTION, WE FURROW OUR BROWS QUIZZICALLY AND SHAKE OUR HEADS. COFFEE KEEPS US AWAKE, IT DOESN'T SEND US TO THE BATHROOM! WELL, FOR ABOUT 29 PERCENT OF COFFEE DRINKERS, COFFEE DOES MAKE US NEED TO DEFECATE WITHIN MINUTES AFTER DRINKING IT. MOREOVER, CAFFEINATED COFFEE INSTIGATES THIS RESPONSE MORE THAN DECAF, HAVING ABOUT THE SAME EFFECT AS A 1000 KCAL MEAL.

This phenomenon hasn't garnered much research attention but it does seem to get discussed quite a bit amongst drinkers (at least, those who respond to it!). Consequently, nobody has researched what it is in coffee that works the magic. We can assume that whatever the chemical is, it is working from a distance. The response can begin in as little as four minutes, suggesting some kind of signal is being translated down to the body's nether regions.

Fortunately, no medical problem is associated with this phenomenon. Either it happens to you or it doesn't. Maybe some people just ought to keep a roll of toilet paper handy, just in case!

WILL DRINKING
= COFFEE =
DEHYDRATE ME?

**THE LITTLE COFFEE
KNOW-IT-ALL**

SOMEWHERE, WE ALL LEARNED THAT CAFFEINE CAUSES US TO URINATE. THIS IS THE MOST PREVALENT BELIEF ABOUT CAFFEINE. IF TRUE, THEN IT IS ALMOST CERTAINLY GOING TO PUT US AT RISK OF DEHYDRATION (WELL, FOR THOSE OF US WHO DRINK IT OFTEN).

We shouldn't really think about whether caffeine alone is a diuretic. After all, we rarely consume caffeine by itself. The vast majority of caffeine consumption is taken in the form of caffeinated beverages, though some people do take caffeine pills just so stay awake.

Thus, we should really be asking if caffeinated beverages, such as coffee, are diuretics.

Once we begin considering caffeinated beverages, doing research to answer this question becomes simple; we can compare drinking them to drinking water. The results of the research help us conclude that caffeinated beverages (a single cup of coffee, for example) don't cause us to urinate any more than water does. Higher doses of caffeine (two to three cups of coffee) may cause a short-term water imbalance, but only if the person has not been drinking coffee for a few days. For even larger volumes of caffeine intake, the research is murky and what does exist is in the context of high-performing athletes. In short, if a person builds up a tolerance to caffeine, caffeinated beverages aren't going to cause urination any more than drinking water would.

Thus, caffeinated beverages don't lead to dehydration. In fact, caffeinated beverages can be included as part of our daily requirement of fluid intake. So drink up and be happy!

REFERENCES
★ ★ ★

Part One: The Beans

100% ARABICA—SO WHAT?

Davis A, Govaerts R, Bridson D, Stoffelen P. 2006. An annotated taxonomic conspectus of the genus *Coffea* (Rubiaceae). Botanical Journal of the Linnean Society. 152(4):465–512.

Davis A, Tosh J, Ruch N, Fay M. 2011. Growing coffee: Psilanthus (Rubiaceae) subsumed on the basis of molecular and morphological data; implications for the size, morphology, distribution and evolutionary history of *Coffea*. Botanical Journal of the Linnean Society. 167(4):4 357–377.

Maurin O, Davis A, Chester M, Mvungi E, Jaufeerally-Fakim Y, Fay M. 2007. Towards a phylogeny for *Coffea* (Rubiaceae): Identifying well-supported lineages based on nuclear and plastid DNA sequences. Annals of Botany. 100(7):1565–1583.

WHAT'S SO IMPORTANT ABOUT HIGH-ALTITUDE COFFEE?

Avelino J, Barboza B, Araya J, Fonseca C, Davrieux F, Guyot B, Cilas C. 2005. Effects of slope exposure, altitude and yield on coffee quality in two altitude terroirs of Costa Rica, Orosi and Santa Maria de Dota. Journal of the Science of Food and Agriculture. 85(11):1869–1876.

Bertrand B, Vaast P, Alpizar E, Etienne H, Davrieux F, Charmetant P. 2006. Comparison of bean biochemical composition and beverage quality of Arabica hybrids involving Sudanese-Ethiopian origins with traditional varieties at various elevations in Central America. Tree Physiology. 26(9):1239–1248.

Cerqueira E, Queiroz D, Pinto F, Santos N, Vale S. 2011. Analysis of the variability in productivity and quality of mountain family coffee farms. Revista Brasileira de Armazenamento. 36(2):119–132.

Guyot B, Gueule D, Manez J, Perriot J, Giron, Villain L. 1996. Influence de l'altitude et del'ombrage sur la qualite des J cafes Arabica. Plantations, Recherche, Developpement. 3(4):272–283.

He C, Davies Jr F, Lacey R. 2007. Separating the effects of hypobaria and hypoxia on lettuce: growth and gas exchange. Physiologia Plantarum. 131(2):226–240.

Franklin K, Wigge P. 2014. Temperature and Plant Development. Hoboken, NJ: Wiley-Blackwell. 240 pp.

Levine L, Bisbee P, Richards J, Birmele M, Prior R, Perchonok M, Dixon M, Yorio N, Stutte G, Wheeler R. 2008. Quality characteristics of the radish grown under reduced atmospheric pressure. Advances in Space Research. 41:754–762.

DaMatta F, Ramalho J. 2006. Impacts of drought and temperature stress on coffee physiology and production—a review. Brazilian Journal of Plant Physiology. 18(1):55–81.

Rajapakse N, He C, Cisneros-Zevallos L, Davies Jr F. 2009. Hypobaria and hypoxia affects growth and phytochemical contents of lettuce. Scientia Horticulturae. 122(2):171–178.

Wehkamp C, Stasiak M, Lawson J, Yorio N, Stutte G, Richards J, Wheeler R, Dixon M. 2012. Radish (*Raphanus sativa* L. cv. Cherry BombII) growth, net carbon exchange rate, and transpiration at decreased atmospheric pressure and/or oxygen. Gravitational and Space Biology. 26(1):3–16.

WHAT'S SO SPECIAL ABOUT SHADE-GROWN COFFEE?

Beer J. 1987. Advantages, disadvantages and desirable characteristics of shade trees for coffee, cacao and tea. Agroforestry Systems. 5(1):3–13.

Muschler R. 1998. Tree-crop compatibility in agroforestry: Production and quality of coffee grown under managed tree shade in Costa Rica [Ph.D. Dissertation]. [University of Florida (FL)]. 219 pages.

Perfecto I, Rice R, Greenberg R, Van der Voort M. 1996. Shade coffee: A disappearing refuge for biodiversity. Bioscience. 46(8):598–608.

Steiman S, Idol T, Bittenbender H, Gautz L. 2011. Shade coffee in Hawai'i–Exploring some aspects of quality, growth, yield, and nutrition. Scientia Horticulturae. 128(2):152–158.

COFFEE IS THE SEED OF A FRUIT?
Braham J, Bressani R, editors. 1979. Coffee pulp: Composition, technology, and utilization. Institute of Nutrition of Central America and Panama (INCAP). 95 pp.

Morris J. 2013. Coffee, a condensed history. In: Thurston, R, Morris J, Steiman S, editors. Coffee: A Comprehensive Guide to the Bean, the Beverage, and the Industry. Lanham, MD: Rowman and Littlefield. 416 pp.

Silva R, Brigatti J, Santos V, Mecina G, Silva L. 2013. Allelopathic effect of the peel of coffee fruit. Scientia Horticulturae. 158(4):39–44.

Wintgens J, editor. 2009. Coffee: Growing, Processing, Sustainable Production. Weinheim, Germany: Wiley-VCH Verlag GmbH. 983 pp.

IS ONE ROUND PEABERRY BETTER THAN TWO FLAT-FACED BEANS?
Bertrand B, Etienne H, Cilas C, Charrier A, Baradat P. 2005. Coffea arabica hybrid performance for yield, fertility and bean weight. Euphytica. 141(3):255–262.

Chandrasekhara M, Narayana B. 1953. Quality and grading in coffee bean-relative merits of peaberry and "A" grade beans. Science and Culture. 18(12):592–3.

Monge F. 1962. Frecuencia de café caracolillo en plantas provenientesde semillas irradiadas. Turrialba. 12:209–210.

Ortiz E, Simon E. 1993. Growth and development of seedlings from misshapen coffee (Coffea Arabica L.) seeds. Part I. Nursery. Cultivos Tropicales. 14(2/3):89–91.

Pimenta T, Pereira R, Correa J, Silva J. 2009. Roasting processing of dry coffee cherry: Influence of grain shape and temperature on physical, chemical, and sensorial grain properties. Curitiba. 27(1):97–106.

Ricketts T, Daily G, Ehrlich P, Michener C. 2004. Economic value of tropical forest to coffee production. Proceedings of the Natural Academy of Sciences of the United States of America. 101(34):12579–12582.

Steiman S, Idol T, Bittenbender H, Guatz L. 2011. Shade coffee in Hawai'i–Exploring some aspects of quality, growth, yield, and nutrition. Scientia Horticulturae. 128(2):152–158.

van der Vossen H. 1985. Coffee Selection and Breeding. In: Clifford M, Willson K, editors. Coffee: Botany, Biochemistry and Production of Beans and Beverage. London, England: Croom Helm, Ltd. p 48–96. pp 457.

WHY DOES MY ROASTER TALK ABOUT CHERRY PROCESSING?
Bytof G, Knopp S-E, Schieberle P, Teutsch I, Selmar D. 2005. Influence of processing on the generation of γ-aminobutyric acid in green coffee beans. European Food Research and Technology. 220(3–4):245–250.

Bytof, G, Knopp S-E, Kramer D, Breitenstein B, Bergervoet J, Groot S, Selmar D. 2007. Transient occurrence of seed germination processes during coffee post-harvest treatment. Annals of Botany. 100(1):61–66.

Coradi P, Borem F, Saath R, Marques E. 2007. Effect of drying and storage conditions on the quality of natural and washed coffee. Coffee Science. Lavaras. 2(1):38–47.

Gonzalez-Rios O, Suarez-Quiroz M, Boulanger R, Barel M, Guyot B, Guiraud J-P, Schorr-Galindo S. 2005. Impact of "ecological" post harvest processing on coffee aroma: II. Roasted coffee. International Journal of Food Microbiology. 103(3):339–345.

Joet T, Laffargue A, Descroix F, Doulbeau S, Bertrand B, de kochko A, Dussert S. 2010. Influence of environmental factors, wet processing and their interactions on the biochemical composition of green Arabica coffee beans. Food Chemistry. 118(3):693–701.

Knopp S, Bytof G, Selmar D. 2006. Influence of processing on the content of sugars in green Arabica coffee beans. European Food Research and Technology. 223:195–201.

Quintero, G. 1999. Infuencia del proceso de beneficio en la calidad del cafe. Cenicafe. 50(1):78–88.

Selmar D, Bytof G, Knopp S-E, Breitenstein B. 2006. Germination of coffee seeds and its significance for coffee quality. Plant Biology. 8(2):260–264.

Tarzia A, Scholz M, Petkowicz C. 2010. Influence of the postharvest processing method on polysaccharides and coffee beverages. International Journal of Food Science & Technology. 45(10):2167–2175.

CAN YOU TELL ME THE FLAVOR PROFILE OF THE COFFEE FROM LOCATION X?

Food and Agriculture Organization of the United Nations. Statistics Division. FAOSTAT. [Accessed 10/27/14]. http://faostat3.fao.org/download/Q/*/E.

International Coffee Organization. [Accessed 10/27/14]. http://www.ico.org/trade_statistics.asp.

Steiman, S. 2013. Why does coffee taste that way? Notes from the field. In: Thurston R, Morris J, Steiman S, editors. Coffee: A Comprehensive Guide to the Bean, the Beverage, and the Industry. Lanham, MD: Rowman & Littlefield. 416 pp.

WHY DOES A COFFEE PLANT PRODUCE CAFFEINE?

Baumann, T. 2006. Some thoughts on the physiology of caffeine in coffee – and a glimpse of metabolite profiling. Brazilian Journal of Plant Physiology. 18(1):243–251.

Filippi SB, Azevedo RA, Sodek L, Mazzafera P. 2007. Allantoin has a limited role as nitrogen source in cultured coffee cells. Journal of Plant Physiology. 164(5):544–552.

Mazzafera P, Yamaoka-Yano D, Vitoria A. 1996. Para que serve a cafeina em plantas? Revista Brasileira de Fisiologia Vegetal. 8(1):67–74.

Wright GA, Baker DD, Palmer MJ, Stabler D, Mustard JA, Power EF, Borland AM, Stevenson PC. 2013. Caffeine in floral nectar enhances a pollinator's memory of reward. Science. 339(6124):1202–1204.

COFFEE CAN RUST?

McCook, S. 2006. Global rust belt: Hemileia vastatrix and the ecological integration of world coffee production since 1850. Journal of Global History. 1(2):177–195.

Muller R, Berry D, Avelino J, Bieysse D. 2009. Coffee Diseases. In: Wintgens J, editor. Coffee: Growing, Processing, Sustainable Production. Germany: Wiley-VCH, p. 495–549.

HOW DO I REALLY KNOW THAT'S KONA COFFEE?

Anderson K, Smith B. 2002. Chemical profiling to differentiate geographic growing origins of coffee. Journal of Agricultural and Food Chemistry. 50(7):2068–2075.

Borsato D, Pina M, Spacino K, Scholz M, Filho A. 2011. Application of artificial neural networks in the geographical identification of coffee samples. European Food Research and Technology. 233:533–543.

Casal S, Oliveira MB, Alves MR, Ferreira MA. 2000. Discriminate analysis of roasted coffee varieties for trigonelline, nicotinic acid, and caffeine content. Journal of Agricultural and Food Chemistry. 48(8):3420–3424.

Coradi P, Borem F, Saath R, Marques E. 2007. Effect of drying and storage conditions on the quality of natural and washed coffee. Coffee Science. 2(1):38–47.

Suarez-Quiroz M, Gonzalez-Rios O, Barel M, Guyot B, Schorr-Galindo S, Guiraud J-P. Effect of the post-harvest processing procedure on OTA occurrence in artificially contaminated coffee. Journal of Food Microbiology. 103(3):339–345.

Guyot B, Gueule D, Manez J-C, Perriot J-J, Giron J, Villain L. 1996. Influence de l'altitude et de l'ombrage sur la qualite des cafes Arabica. Plantations, recherche, developpement. Juillet-Aout. 3(4):272–283.

Knopp S, Bytof G, Selmar D. 2006. Influence of processing on the content of sugars in green Arabica coffee beans. European Food Research and Technology. 223:195–201.

Lopez-Galilea I, Fournier N, Cid C, Guichard E. 2006. Changes in headspace volatile concentrations of coffee brews caused by the roasting process and the brewing procedure. Journal of Agricultural and Food Chemistry. 2006. 54(22):8560–8566.

Montavon P, Duruz E, Rumo G, Pratz G. 2003. Evolution of green coffee protein profiles with maturation and relationship to coffee cup quality. Journal of Agricultural and Food Chemistry. 51(8):2328–2334.

Ozdestan O, van Ruth S, Alewijn M, Koot A, Romano A, Cappellin L, Biasioli F. 2013. Differentiation of specialty coffees by proton transfer reaction-mass spectrometry. Food Research International. 53(1):433–439.

Risticevic S, Carasek E, Pawliszyn J. 2008. Headspace solid-phase microextraction–gaschromatographic–time-of-flight mass spectrometric methodology for geographical origin verification of coffee. Analytica Chimca Acta. 617(1–2):72–84.

Rocha S, Maeztu L, Barros A, Cid C, Coimbra MA. 2003. Screening and distinction of coffee brews based on headspace solid phase microextraction/gas chromatography/principal component analysis. Journal of the Science of Food and Agriculture. 84(1):43–51.

Rodrigues C, Brunner M, Steiman S, Bowen G, Nogueira J, Gautz L, Prohaska T, Maguas C. 2011. Isotopes as tracers of the Hawaiian coffee-producing regions. Journal of Agricultural and Food Chemistry. 59(18):10239–10246.

Wang N, Fu Y, Lim LT. 2011. Feasibility study on chemometric discrimination of roasted Arabica coffees by solvent extraction and Fourier transform infrared spectroscopy. Journal of Agricultural and Food Chemistry. 59(7):3220–3226.

Weckerle B, Richling E, Heinrich S, Schreier P. 2002. Origin assessment of green coffee (Coffea arabica) by multi-element stable isotope analysis of caffeine. Analytical and Bioanalytical Chemistry. 374(5):886–890.

THAT COFFEE WAS EATEN BY AN ANIMAL?

Cheong M, Tong K, Ong J, Liu S, Curran P, Yu B. 2013. Volatile composition and antioxidant capacity of Arabica coffee. Food Research International. 51(1):388–396.

Jumhawan U, Putri S, Yusianto, Marwani E, Bamba T, Fukusaki E. 2013. Selection of discriminant markers for authentication of Asian palm civet coffee (Kopi Luwak): A metabolomics approach. Journal of Agricultural and Food Chemistry. 61(33):7994–8001.

Marcone, M. 2004. Composition and properties of Indonesian palm civet coffee (Kopi Luwak) and Ethiopian civet coffee. Food Research International. 37(9):901–912.

Ozdestan O, van Ruth S, Alewijn M, Koot A, Romano A, Cappellin L, Biasioli F. 2013. Differentiation of specialty coffees by proton transfer reaction-mass spectrometry. Food Research International. 53(1):433–439.

Lynn G, Rogers C. Civet cat coffee's animal cruelty secrets. 2013. BBC News, London. [Accessed 10/21/14]. http://www.bbc.com/news/uk-england-london-24034029.

Part Two: The Roast

WHY IS A COFFEE BEAN JUST A TINY TEST TUBE?

Baggenstoss J, Poisson L, Kaegi R, Perren R, Escher F. 2008. Coffee roasting and aroma formation: Application of different time-temperature conditions. Journal of Agricultural and Food Chemistry. 56(14):5836–5846.

Czerny M, Mayer F, Grosch W. 1999. Sensory study on the character impact odorants of roasted Arabica coffee. Journal of Agricultural and Food Chemistry. 47(2):695–699.

Schenker S, Heinemann C, Huber M, Pompizzi R, Perren R, Escher R. 2002. Impact of roasting conditions on the formation of aroma compounds in coffee beans. Journal of Food Science. 67(1):60–66.

Flament I. 2002. Coffee Flavor Chemistry. Chichester, England: John Wiley & Sons, Ltd. 410 pp.

Mayer F, Czerny M, Grosch W. 2000. Sensory study of the character impact aroma compounds of a coffee beverage. European Food Research and Technology. 211(4):272–276.

Ryan D, Shellie R, Tranchida P, Casilli A, Mondello L, Marriott P. 2004. Analysis of roasted coffee bean volatiles by using comprehensive two-dimensional gas chromatography–time-of-flight mass spectrometry. Journal of Chromatography A. 1054(1–2):57–65.

Sunarharum W, Williams D, Smyth H. 2014. Complexity of coffee flavor: A compositional and sensory perspective. Food Research International. 62:315–325.

ARE YOU AFRAID OF DARK ROASTS?

Bekedam E, Loots M, Schols H, Boekel M, Smit G. 2008. Roasting effects on formation mechanisms of coffee brew melanoidins. Journal of Agricultural and Food Chemistry. 56(16):7138–7145.

Bhumiratana N, Adhikari K, Chambers IV E. 2011. Evolution of sensory aroma attributes from coffee beans to brewed coffee. LWT – Food Science and Technology. 44(10):2185–2192.

Charles-Bernard M, Kraehenbuehl K, Rytz A, Roberts DD. 2005. Interactions between volatile and nonvolatile coffee components. 1. Screening of nonvolatile components. Journal of Agricultural and Food Chemistry. 53(11):4417–4425.

International Coffee Organization.1991. Sensory study of the effect of degree of roast and brewing formula on the final cup characteristics. Chapter 7 of Quality Series. International Coffee Organization. 16 pp.

Rubach M, Lang R, Bytof G, Stiebitz H, Lantz I, Hofmann T, Somoza V. 2014. A dark brown roast coffee blend is less effective at stimulating gastric acid secretion in healthy volunteers compared to a medium roast market blend. Molecular Nutrition & Food Research. 58(6):1370–1373.

Strezov V, Evans T. 2005. Thermal analysis of the reactions kinetics of green coffee during roasting. International Journal of Food Properties. 8(1):101–111.

Sualeh A, Endris S, Mohammed A. 2014. Processing method, variety and roasting effect on cup quality of Arabica coffee (Coffea arabica L.). Discourse Journal of Agriculture and Food Sciences. 2(2):70–75.

WHAT DO YOU MEAN BY COFFEE FRESHNESS?

Anese M, Manzocco L, Nicoli M. 2006. Modeling the secondary shelf-life of ground roasted coffee. Journal of Agricultural and Food Chemistry. 54(15):5571–5576.

Kreuml M, Majchrzak D, Ploederl B, Koenig J. 2013. Changes in sensory quality characteristics of coffee during storage. Food Science & Nutrtion. 1(4):267–272.

Marin K, Požrl T, Zlatic E, Plestenjak A. 2008. A new aroma index to determine the aroma quality ofroasted and ground coffee during storage. Food Technology and Biotechnology. 46(4):442–447.

Ross C, Pecka K, Weller K. 2006. Effect of storage conditions on the sensory quality of ground Arabica coffee. Journal of Food Quality. 29(6):596–606.

Toci A, Neto V, Torres A, Farah A. 2013. Changes in triacylglycerols and free fatty acids composition during storage of roasted coffee. LWT - Food Science and Technology. 50(2):581–590.

Xiuju Wang X, Lim L-T. 2014. Effect of roasting conditions on carbon dioxide degassing behavior in coffee. Food Research International. 61:144–151.

Yeretzian C, Pascual E, Goodman B. 2012. Effect of roasting conditions and grinding on free radical contents of coffee beans stored in air. Food Chemistry. 131(3):811–816.

HOW DO I KEEP MY COFFEE FRESH?
Gloss A, Schonbachler B, Rast M, Deuber L, Yeretzian C. 2014. Freshness indices of roasted coffee: Monitoring the loss of freshness for single serve capsules and roasted whole beans in different packaging. Chimia. 68(3):179–182.

HOW IS COFFEE DECAFFEINATE?
Bee S, Brando C, Brumen G, Carvalhaes N, Kolling-Speer I, Speer K, Liverani F, Teixeira A, Teixeira R, Thomaziello R, Viani R, Vitzthum O. 2005. The Raw Bean. In: Illy A. Viani R, editors. Espresso Coffee, Second Edition: The Science of Quality. Amsterdam: Elsevier Academic Press. p. 87–178.

Ramalakshmi K, Raghavan B. 1999. Caffeine in coffee: its removal. why and how? Critical Reviews in Food Science and Nutrition. 39(5):441–456.

WILL A DARK ROAST KEEP ME UP AT NIGHT?
de Moura SC, Germer S, Anjos V, Mori E, Mattoso L, Firmino A, and Nascimento CJ. 2007. Influence of roasting parameters on the physical, chemical and sensory characteristics of pure Arabica coffee. Brazilian Journal of Food Technology. 10(1):17–25.

Rodarte M, Abrahao S, Pereira R, Malta M. 2009. Non-volatile compounds in coffee from the south of Minas Gerais state region submitted to different roasting degrees. Ciencia e Agrotecnologia 33(5):1366–1371.

Sigma-Aldrich. 1999. Product information sheet for product number C0750: caffeine (anhydrous).

de Siqueira H. de Abreu C. 2006. Physical-chemical composition and quality of coffee submitted to two roasting procedures and to different methods of preparation. Cienciae Agrotecnologia. 30(1):112–117.

Steiman, S. Unpublished data.

Tfouni S, Serrate C, Carreiro L, Camargo M, Teles C, Cipolli K, Furlani R. 2012. Effect of roasting on chlorogenic acids, caffeine and polycyclic aromatic hydrocarbons levels in two Coffea cultivars: Coffea arabica cv. Catuai Amarelo IAC-62 and Coffea canephora cv. Apoata IAC-2258. International Journal of Food Science and Technology. 47(2):406–415.

WHAT'S THE DEAL WITH ACRYLAMIDE?
Acrylamide, ICSC 0091. [Accessed 11/6/2014]. http://www. ilo.org/dyn/icsc/showcard.display?p_card_id=0091.

Alves R, Soares C, Casal S, Fernandes J, Oliveira M. 2010. Acrylamide in espresso coffee: Influence of species, roast degree and brew length. Food Chemistry. 119(3):929–934.

Baum M, Bohm N, Gorlitz J, Lantz I, Merz KH, Ternite R, Eisenbrand G. 2008. Fate of ^{14}C-acrylamide in roasted and ground coffee during storage. Molecular Nutrition and Food Research. 52(5):600–608.

Capuano E, Fogliano V. 2011. Acrylamide and 5-hydroxymethylfurfural (HMF): A review on metabolism, toxicity, occurrence in food and mitigation strategies. LWT - Food Science and Technology. 44(4):793–810.

Chu Y, editor. 2012. Coffee: Emerging Health Effects and Disease Prevention. Ames, IA: Wiley-Blackwell. 354 pp.

IS THERE MORE TO KNOW IF I'M A HOME ROASTER?
Quintero, G. 1999. Infuencia del proceso de beneficio en la calidad del cafe. Cenicafe. 50(1):78–88.

Ribeiro F, Borem F, Giomo G, de Lima R, Malta M, Figueiredo L. 2011. Storage of green coffee in hermetic packaging injected with CO2. Journal of Stored Products Research. 47(4):341–348.

Scheidig C, Czerny M, Schieberle P. 2007. Changes in key odorants of raw coffee beans during storage under defined conditions. Journal of Agricultural and Food Chemistry. 55(14):5768–5775.

Part Three: The Brew

BREWING PARAMETER: ENERGY (TEMPERATURE)

Andueza S, Maeztu L, Pascual L, Ibanez C, Paz de Pena M, Cid C. 2003. Influence of extraction temperature on the final quality of espresso coffee. Journal of the Science of Food and Agriculture. 83(3):240–248.

Bladyka E. 2013. The Coffee Brewing Institute: Setting the Stage for Specialty Coffee. The Specialty Coffee Chronical. [Accessed 9/3/14]. http://www.scaa.org/chronicle/2013/10/04/the-coffeebrewing-institute/.

International Coffee Organization. 1991. Sensory and chemical assessment of coffee brewing conditions. Chapter 9 of Quality Series. International Coffee Organization. 33 pp.

BREWING PARAMETER: WATER QUALITY

Hendon C, Colonna-Dashwood L, Colonna-Dashwood M. 2014. The role of dissolved cations in coffee extraction. Journal of Agricultural and Food Chemistry. 62(21):4947–4950.

International Coffee Organization. 1991. Sensory study of the effect of water type on the sensory quality of brewed coffee. Chapter 8 of Quality Series. 17 pp.

Navarini L, Rivetti D. 2010. Water quality for espresso coffee. Food Chemistry. 122(2):424–428.

Pangborn R, Trabue I, Little A. 1971. Analysis of coffee, tea and artificially flavoured drinks prepared from mineralized waters. Journal of Food Science. 36(2):355–362.

Lockhart E, Tucker C, Merritt M. 1955. The effect of water impurities on the flavor of brewed coffee. Journal of Food Science. 20(6):598–605.

BREWING PARAMETER: SURFACE AREA

Andueza S, de Pena MP, Cid C. 2003. Chemical and sensorial characteristics of espresso coffee as affected by grinding and torre factoroast. Journal of Agricultural and Food Chemistry. 51(24):7034–7039.

International Coffee Organization. 1991. Sensory and chemical assessment of coffee brewing conditions. Chapter 9 of Quality Series. International Coffee Organization. 33 pp.

BREWING PARAMETER: BREW RATIO

International Coffee Organization. 1991. Sensory study of the effect of degree of roast and brewing formula on the final cup characteristics. Chapter 7 of Quality Series. International Coffee Organization. 16 pp.

BREWING PARAMETER: CONTACT TIME

International Coffee Organization. 1991. Sensory and chemical assessment of coffee brewing conditions. Chapter 9 of Quality Series. International Coffee Organization. 33 pp.

Pangborn, R. 1982. Influence of water composition, extraction procedures, and holding time and temperature on quality of coffee beverage. Lebensmittel-Wissenschaft & Technologie. 15(3):151–168.

BREWING PARAMETER: FILTER TYPE

Srebernich S, Vicente E, Franceschini S, Minatel L. 2009. Effect of filter type on the caffeine contents in the coffee beverages. Revista do Instituto Adolfo Lutz. 68(1):29–33.

WHY CAN'T I CALL IT A SIPHON BREWER?

Bersten I. 1993. Coffee Floats, Tea Sinks. Sydney, Austrailia: Helian Books. p. 83.

HOW DO I GET THE MOST BUZZ FROM A CUP?

Andueza S, de Pena MP, Cid C. 2003. Chemical and sensorial characteristics of espresso coffee as affected by grinding and torrefacto roast. Journal of Agricultural and Food Chemistry. 51(24):7034–7039.

Bell L, Wetzel C, Grand A. 1996. Caffeine content in coffee as influenced by grinding and brewing techniques. Food Research International. 29(8):785–789.

Budryn G, Nebesny E, Podsedek A, Żyżelewicz D, Materska M, Jankowski S, Janda B. 2009. Effect of different extraction methods on the recovery of chlorogenic acids, caffeine and Maillard reaction products in coffee beans. European Food Research and Technology. 228:913–922.

Caporaso N, Genovese A, Canela M, Civitella A, Sacchi R. 2014. Neapolitan coffee brew chemical analysis in comparison to espresso, moka and American brews. Food Research International. 61:152–160.

Sigma-Aldrich. 1999. Product information sheet for product number C0750: caffeine (anhydrous).

Silvarolla M, Mazzafera P, Alves de Lima M. 2000. Caffeine content of Ethiopian *Coffea Arabica* beans. Genetics and Molecular Biology. 23(1):213–215.

Srebernich S, Vicente E, Franceschini S, Minatel A. 2009. Effect of filter type on the caffeine contents in the coffee beverages. Revista do Instituto Adolfo Lutz. 68(1):29–33.

Steiman, S. Unpublished data.

WHY DOES YOUR COFFEE TASTE DIFFERENT THAN IT DID LAST TIME?

Bridge D, Voss J. 2014. Hippocampal binding of novel information with dominant memory traces can support both memory stability and change. The Journal of Neuroscience. 34(6):2203–2213.

Cappuccio R, Teixeira A, Teixeira R. 2006. The effect of black bean, black-green bean and immature bean defects in espresso coffee: one single bean can spoil one cup. Presented at: 21st ASIC International Conference on Coffee Science; Montpellier, France. 11–15 September, 2006. p. 368-378.

Chan K, Tong E, Tan D, Koh A. 2013. What do love and jealousy taste like? Emotion. 13(6):1142–1149.

Oberfeld D, Hecht H, Allendorf U, Wickelmaier F. 2009. Ambient lighting modifies the flavor of wine. Journal of Sensory Studies. 24(6):797–832.

Piqueras-Fiszman B, Alcaide J, Roura E, Spence C. 2012. Is it the plate or is it the food? Assessing the influence of the color (black or white) and shape of the plate on the perception of the food placed on it. Food Quality and Preference. 24(1):205–208.

Piqueras-Fiszman, B, Laughlin Z, Miodownik M, Spence C. 2012. Tasting spoons: Assessing how the material of a spoon affects the taste of the food. Food Quality and Preference. 24(1):24–29.

Piqueras-Fiszman B, Spence C. 2012. The influence of the color of the cup on consumers' perception of a hot beverage. Journal of Sensory Studies. 27(5):324–331.

Piqueras-Fiszman B, Spence C. 2012. The influence of the feel of product packaging on the perception of the oral-somatosensory texture of food. Food Quality and Preference. 26(1):67–73.

Piqueras-Fiszman B, Spence C. 2014. Colour, pleasantness, and consumption behaviour within a meal. Appetite. 75:165–172.

Platte P, Herbert C, Pauli P, Breslin PAS. 2013. Oral perceptions of fat and taste stimuli are modulated by affect and mood induction. PLOSOne. 8(6):e65006. doi:10.1371/journal.pone.0065006.

Schacter D. 2008. Searching for memory: The brain, the mind, and the past. New York, NY: Basic Books. 417 pp.

Spence C. 2012. Auditory contributions to flavour perception and feeding behavior. Physiology & Behavior. 107(4):505–515.

Velasco C, Jones R, King S, Spence C. 2013. Assessing the influence of the multisensory environment on the whisky drinking experience. Flavour. 2(23):1–11.

HOW CAN I OUTSMART MY OWN HEAD?

Brochet F, Morror G, Dubourdieu D. 2001. The color of odors. Brain and Language. 79(2):309–320.

Brochet F, Morrot G. 1999. Influence of the context on the perception of wine—Cognitive and methodological implications. Journal International des Sciences de la Vigne et du Vin. 33(4):187–192.

Lawless H, Heymann H. 1998. Sensory Evaluation of Food: Principles and Practices. New York, NY: Kluwer Academic Press. 827 pp.

Meilgaard M, Civille G, Carr B. 1987. Sensory Evaluation Techniques. Boca Raton, FL: CRC Press, Inc. 281 pp.

Stone H, Sidel J. 1985. Sensory Evaluation Practices. Orlando, FL: Academic Press, Inc. 326 pp.

HOW COME MY TEXTBOOK GOT THE TONGUE MAP WRONG?

Bartoshuk L. 1993. Genetic and pathological taste variation: What can we learn from animal models and human disease? In: CIBA Foundation Symposium. The Molecular Basis of Smell and Taste Transduction. Chichester, England: John Wiley & Sons. p 251–267.

Boring E. 1942. Sensation and Perception in the History of Experimental Psychology. New York, NY: Appleton Century Crofts. 613 pp.

Chaudhari N, Roper S. 2010. The cell biology of taste. The Journal of Cell Biology. 190(3):285–296.

Collings V. 1974. Human taste response as a function of locus of stimulation on the tongue and soft palate. Perception & Psychophysics. 16(1):169–174.

Hanig D. 1901. Zur Psychophysik des Geschmackssinnes. Philosophische Studien 17. P. 576–623.

Ikeda K. 2002. New seasonings. Translation of original 1909 paper. Chemical Senses. 27(9):847–849.

Lawless H, Heymann H. 1998. Sensory Evaluation of Food: Principles and Practices. Kluwer Academic Press, New York. 827 pp.

Lindemann B, Ogiwara Y, Ninomiya Y. 2002. The discovery of umami. Chemical Senses. 27(9):843–844.

IS THAT CHEESE IN MY COFFEE?

Lucey J. 2004. Formation, structural properties and rheology of acid-coagulated milk gels. In: Fox P, McSweeney P, Cogan T, Guinee T, editors. Cheese: Chemistry, Physics & Microbiology, Vol 1, Third Edition: General Aspects. Academic Press. 640 pp.

Yuan Y, Velev O, Chen K, Campbell B, Kaler E, Lenhoff A. 2002. Effect of pH and $Ca^{2}+$- induced associations of soybean proteins. Journal of Agricultural and Food Chemistry. 50(17):4953–4958.

CAN I DRINK COFFEE WHEN I'M IN OUTER SPACE?

Yirka B. Italians to Send ISSpresso Machine to ISS. 2014. Phys Org. [Accessed 10/27/14]. http://phys.org/news/2014-06-italians-isspresso-machine-iss. html.

Phillips T. The Zero Gravity Coffee Cup. 2013. National Aeronautics and Space Administration (NASA): Science News. [Accessed 10/27/14]. http://science.nasa.gov/science-news/science-at-nasa/2013/15jul_coffeecup/.

Students Solve Space Coffee Problem. 2008. The Telegraph. [Accessed 10/27/14]. http://www.telegraph.co.uk/news/newstopics/howaboutthat/3207735/Students-solve-space-coffee-problem.html.

WHY DOES COFFEE SEND ME STRAIGHT TO THE BATHROOM?

Boekema PJ, Samsom M, van Berge Henegouwen G, Smout AJ. 1999. Coffee and gastrointestinal function: facts and fiction. A review. Scandinavian Journal of Gastroenterology. 230(Supplement):35–39.

WILL DRINKING COFFEE DEHYDRATE ME?

Armstrong LE. 2002. Caffeine, body fluid-electrolyte balance, and exercise performance. International Journal of Sport Nutrition and Exercise Metabolism. 12(2):189–206.

Maughan RJ, Griffin J. 2003. Caffeine ingestion and fluid balance: a review. Journal of Human Nutrition and Dietetics. 16(6):411–420.

DID YOU KNOWS

Page 25: Mekonnen M, Hoekstra A. 2011. The green, blue and grey water footprint of crops and derived crop products. Hydrology and Earth System Sciences. 15(5):1577–1600.

Page 29: Nkondjock, A. 2012. Coffee cancers. In: Chu Y, editor. Coffee: Emerging Health Effects and Disease Prevention. Ames, IA: Wiley-Blackwell. 352 pp.

Page 44: Jenkins R, Stageman N, Fortune C, Chuck C. 2014. Effect of the type of bean, processing, and geographical location on the biodiesel produced from waste coffee grounds. Energy Fuels. 28(2):1166–1174.

Page 44: Sampaio A, Dragone G, Vilanova M, Oliveira J, Teixeira J, Mussatto S. 2013. Production, chemical characterization, and sensory profile of a novel spirit elaborated from spent coffee ground. LWT - Food Science and Technology. 54(2):557–563.

Page 49: Stafford-Fraser Q. 2001. On site: The Life and Times of the First Web cam. Communications of the ACM. 44(7):25–26.

Page 76: Lim J, Tan E. 2012. Coffee and Parkinson's disease. In: Chu Y, editor. Coffee: Emerging Health Effects and Disease Prevention. Ames, IA: Wiley-Blackwell. pp 352.

Page 76: Lindsay J, Carmichael P-H, Kroger E, D Laurin. 2012. Coffee and Alzheimer's disease: Epidemiologic evidence. In: Chu Y, editor. Coffee: Emerging Health Effects and Disease Prevention. Ames, IA: Wiley-Blackwell. 352 pp.

Page 76: Matusheski N, Bidel S, Tuomilehto J. 2012. Coffee and Type 2 diabetes risk. In: Chu Y, editor. Coffee: Emerging Health Effects and Disease Prevention. Ames, IA: Wiley-Blackwell. 352 pp.

Page 79: Muriel P, Arauz J. 2012. Coffee and liver health. In: Chu Y, editor. Coffee: Emerging Health Effects and Disease Prevention. Ames, IA: Wiley-Blackwell. 354 pp.

Page 81: United Nations Conference on Trade and Development (UNCTAD). [Accessed 12/8/14]. http://unctadstat. unctad.org/wds/ReportFolders/reportFolders.aspx.

Page 99: Morris J. 2013. The Espresso Menu: An International History. In: Thurston R, Morris J, Steiman S, editors. Coffee: A Comprehensive Guide to the Bean, the Beverage, and the Industry. Lanham, MD: Rowman & Littlefield Publishers. p. 262–278. 416 pp.

Page 102: Johann Friedrich Meyer, Jr., Ludwig Roselius, Karl Heinrich Wimmer, inventors; Preparation of Coffee. 1908 Sept 01. United States Patent 897840.

Page 111: Food and Agriculture Organization of the United Nations: Statistics Division. FAOSTAT. [Accessed 12/8/14]. Faostat3.fao.org/home/E.

ACKNOWLEDGMENTS

★ ★ ★

If you've ever tried to write anything for anybody else to read, you know that it is rarely successful without the help of others, some of whom help in ways you never imagined you would need. For me, this claim is especially true, which arguably makes this the most important page of this book! I am grateful beyond measure to Julia Wieting, who cooked, cleaned, generally took care of me, and brewed much of the coffee while I tried to stand on the shoulders of giants. I am indebted to Spencer Turer for making sure I didn't miss any important bits about brewing parameters, though, like the Godfather, I'm sure one day he'll ask for a favor in return.

While we often joke about just having it piled higher and deeper in academia, there are several professional scientists to whom gratitude is due, for without them checking my work, I would certainly have misstepped. Thank you Dr. H.C. "Skip" Bittenbender, my mentor and friend, for reading through the book and making insightful comments. Thank you, Dr. Mel Jackson, my favourite chemist, for teaching me a great deal about chemistry. Thank you, Dr. Rafael Jimenez-Flores, for helping a complete stranger learn about milk chemistry. And thank you, Dr. Christopher Hendon, for influencing the way I—and the specialty coffee industry—are thinking about water.

ABOUT THE AUTHOR

★ ★ ★

According to his mother, Shawn was drinking coffee as a toddler. Shawn's scientific pursuit of coffee began at Oberlin College and was finely tuned at the University of Hawai'i at Mānoa, where he conducted research within various coffee science disciplines for his MS and PhD degrees.

In addition to this book, Shawn has written *The Hawai'i Coffee Book: A Gourmet's Guide from Kona to Kaua'i* (Watermark Publishing, 2008). He is also a co-editor and author of *Coffee: A Comprehensive Guide to the Bean, the Beverage, and the Industry* (Rowman and Littlefield, 2013). He has published widely in scientific journals, coffee trade journals, newspapers, blogs, and newsletters.

Shawn owns Coffea Consulting, an international consulting company that works within every stage of the coffee industry, from farmers to consumers. He is also co-owner and Chief Science Officer of Daylight Mind Coffee Company, a coffee pub and school.

Shawn is fortunate to live in Hawai'i with his blissful wife, Julia. Aside from cogitating about coffee, he enjoys reading, all manner of whisky, science fiction, and gardening.

INDEX

★ ★ ★